HTML B

Third Edition

Karl Barksdale
Technology Consultant, Provo, Utah
E. Shane Turner
Software Engineer, Orem, Utah

THOMSON
COURSE TECHNOLOGY

Australia • Canada • Mexico • Singapore • Spain • United Kingdom • United States

THOMSON
COURSE TECHNOLOGY

HTML BASICS, Third Edition
by Karl Barksdale and E. Shane Turner

Vice President, School Publishing and Marketing
Cheryl Costantini

Product Manager
David Rivera

Editorial Assistant
Justine Brennan

Director of Production
Patty Stephan

Senior Acquisitions Editor
Jane Mazares

Senior Marketing Manager
Kim Ryttel

School Market Specialist
Meagan Putney

Development Editor
Custom Editorial Productions, Inc.

Production Editor
Custom Editorial Productions, Inc.

Compositor
GEX Publishing Services

Printer
Banta—Menasha

COPYRIGHT © 2005 Course Technology, a division of Thomson Learning, Inc. Thomson Learning™ is a trademark used herein under license.

Printed in the United States of America

2 3 4 5 6 7 8 9 BM 09 08 07 06

For more information, contact Course Technology, 25 Thomson Place, Boston, Massachusetts, 02210.

Or find us on the World Wide Web at: www.course.com

ALL RIGHTS RESERVED. No part of this work covered by the copyright hereon may be reproduced or used in any form or by any means—graphic, electronic, or mechanical, including photocopying, recording, taping, Web distribution, or information storage and retrieval systems—without the written permission of the publisher.

For permission to use material from this text or product, contact us by

Tel (800) 730-2214
Fax (800) 730-2215
www.thomsonrights.com

Disclaimer
Course Technology reserves the right to revise this publication and make changes from time to time in its content without notice.

ISBN-13: 978-0-619-26626-4
ISBN-10: 0-619-26626-0

Get Back to the Basics...
With these *exciting new products*

Our exciting new series of short, programming and application suite books will provide everything needed to learn this software. Other books include:

NEW! HTML and JavaScript BASICS, 3rd Ed. by Barksdale and Turner
20+ hours of instruction for beginning through intermediate learners

0-619-26625-2	Textbook, softcover
0-619-26628-7	Instructor Resources
0-619-26629-5	Review Pack (Data CD)

NEW! HTML, JavaScript, and Advanced Internet Technologies by Barksdale and Turner
35+ hours of instruction for beginning through intermediate learners

0-619-26627-9	Textbook, softcover
0-619-26628-7	Instructor Resources
0-619-26629-5	Review Pack (Data CD)

Programming BASICS, Using Microsoft Visual Basic, C++, HTML, and Java
by Knowlton & Barksdale
35+ hours of instruction for beginning through intermediate learners

0-619-05803-X	Textbook, hardcover
0-619-05801-3	Textbook, softcover
0-619-05802-1	Instructor Resources
0-619-05800-5	Activities Workbook
0-619-05949-4	Review Pack (Data CD)

Internet BASICS by Barksdale, Rutter, & Teeter
35+ hours of instruction for beginning through intermediate learners

0-619-05905-2	Textbook, softcover, spiral-bound
0-619-05906-0	Instructor Resources

NEW! Microsoft Office 2003 BASICS by Pasewark and Pasewark
35+ hours of instruction for beginning through intermediate learners

0-619-18335-7	Textbook, hardcover, spiral-bound
0-619-18337-3	Instructor Resources
0-619-18336-5	Activities Workbook
0-619-18338-1	Review Pack (Data CD)

Join Us On the Internet **www.course.com**

TABLE OF CONTENTS

xiii How to Use This Book
vii Preface
xi Guide for Using This Book

UNIT 1 HTML BASICS

3	**Lesson 1: Quick HTML Know-How**
3	Communicating on the Web
9	Enter Your Mystery Tags the Old-Fashioned Way
11	Save and View Your HTML Page
16	Using Headings
19	Numbered and Bulleted Lists
25	Summary
33	**Lesson 2: HTML Organization Techniques**
33	Creating Better Web Pages
38	Lines and Background Colors
42	Hyperlinks Inside Your Document
46	Creating Hypertext Links to the Web
51	Linking to Pages You Have Already Created
54	Coloring Text
57	Summary

UNIT 1 HTML BASICS

63	**Lesson 3: HTML Power Techniques**
63	The Exciting Web
67	Downloading and Inserting Graphics
73	Pictures of All Sizes
78	Orderly Tables
83	Extraordinary Extras
86	Summary
91	**Lesson 4: HTML Structural Design Techniques**
91	Creating an HTML Frame Set
94	Creating a Navigation Bar
96	Creating a Web Site Welcome Page
97	Creating a Nested Frame Set
99	Creating a Title Bar
101	Using Advanced HTML Options
105	Summary
111	Unit Review

121	**Glossary**
125	**Index**

Preface

Everyone knows how popular the Internet is, but very few people know why. The technologies that make the Internet work have been in existence for over three decades. So why did the Web suddenly become an overnight success?

The Internet owes its tremendous growth to Hypertext Markup Language, or HTML. HTML is a relatively simple method of making documents and online content look great! HTML gives the Web eye-catching appeal. In 1995, many powerful businesses took notice and realized they could advertise, promote their products, or even sell their products online—the rush to develop online Web sites began.

HTML is the backbone of the World Wide Web. It is the primary mechanism used to distribute data across the information superhighway. Learning the capabilities and the structure of HTML is an essential step for anyone who would like to create colorful Web pages like those developed by professional Web designers.

Fortunately, HTML is relatively easy to learn, can be created with a standard text editor or word processor, and works on nearly any type computer system. These are additional reasons why the Web and HTML became so popular so very quickly.

Course Technology is recognized as a leader in Internet-related instruction. Our mission is to change the way people teach and learn technology. In the last ten years, HTML has had the same colossal impact on society as Gutenberg's printing press over 500 years ago. It creates the structure that all other innovative Web technologies are built upon, and it's a tool you should learn. With this book, you will change how you view the Internet and gain a perspective on how you can contribute in a positive way to the Web.

Organization and Features of the Text

HTML BASICS has been written so that HTML skills can be developed quickly and easily. The Step-by-Step sections are fully illustrated and are easy to follow, allowing you to master the basics of the language of the Web, namely HTML.

The text is divided into four interactive hands-on lessons:

Lesson 1—Quick HTML Know-How introduces the basic structure of HTML and will allow you to create your first basic Web page.

Lesson 2—HTML Organization Techniques teaches you how to format Web pages and gives you the techniques required to create hypertext links.

Lesson 3—HTML Power Techniques teaches you how to insert graphics, integrate tables, and manipulate the size, style, and color of fonts.

Lesson 4—HTML Structural Design Techniques teaches you how you can have several Web pages and navigation systems working together. These skills will prove very valuable as you progress to additional Web design tutorials such as *Web Design BASICS*, or texts on JavaScript, Dreamweaver, FrontPage, or other advanced tutorials.

HTML BASICS steps through the basics of HTML literacy. Each lesson includes the following:

- Lesson objectives to specify learning goals.
- Estimated time of completion.
- Vocabulary to introduce new terms used in the lesson.
- Step-by-Step exercises that teach the basics you need to know.
- Screen illustrations that provide visual reinforcement of what you're learning.
- Sidebars with Internet tips related to the lesson topics.
- Special features such as Internet Milestone and Netiquette which provide information about Net history; as well as exciting descriptions of technological career opportunities.
- SCANS correlations.

The end-of-lesson exercises focus on the reinforcement of the skills you have learned in the lesson and provide a comprehensive review of ways you can apply your skills. The end of lesson features include the following:

- Lesson summary.
- Vocabulary review of the new terms presented in the lesson.
- Review questions to assess your comprehension of what you have studied.
- Projects for applying the concepts learned in the lesson.
- Critical Thinking activities that require you to analyze and express your own ideas on a variety of HTML challenges.

The unit review is designed to evaluate your overall comprehension of the lessons. The unit review includes the following:

- HTML tags and attributes command summaries.
- Review questions.
- Cross-curricular activities that apply HTML skills in the areas of language arts, science, social studies, and math.
- Special SCANS projects to help you master the skills you have learned.
- Career simulation activities that will help you apply your HTML skills to job-related situations.

A glossary is provided at the end of the text to provide you with definitions for those tricky HTML tags and terms we all need to learn.

Acknowledgements

Thanks to Cheryl Costantini, Jane Mazares, Kim Ryttel, Dave Rivera, Justine Brennan and the rest of the team at Course Technology. Thanks also to Rose Marie Kuebbing and Ericka McIntyre at Custom Editorial Productions, Inc., for managing the development and production of this book.

Guide for Using This Book

Software

Internet Explorer or Netscape Navigator to view Web pages.

Windows Notepad or Macintosh SimpleText to create HTML documents.

Each of these tools currently comes installed on nearly all standard computers. You may substitute Notepad or SimpleText for a word processor capable of saving text files as .htm or .html documents.

Instructor Resource Kit CD-ROM

The *Instructor Resource Kit* CD-ROM contains a wealth of instructional material you can use to prepare for teaching this course. The CD-ROM stores the following information:

- The solution files for this course.

- ExamView® tests for each lesson. ExamView is a powerful testing software package that enables instructors to create and administer printed, computer (LAN-based), and Internet exams. ExamView includes hundreds of questions that correspond to the topics covered in this text, enabling learners to generate detailed study guides that include page references for further review. The computer-based and Internet testing components enable learners to take exams at their computers and instructors to save time by automatically grading each exam.

- Electronic *Instructor's Manual* that includes instructor lesson plans, student study guides, SCANS correlation, scheduling suggestions, answers to the lesson and unit review questions, and references to the solutions for Step-by-Step exercises, end-of-lesson activities, and Unit Review projects.

- Copies of the figures that appear in the student text, which can be used to prepare transparencies.

- Additional instructional information about individual learning strategies, portfolios, and career planning, and a sample Internet contract.

- PowerPoint presentations showing HTML and other features for each lesson in the text.

SCANS

The Secretary's Commission on Achieving Necessary Skills (SCANS) from the U.S. Department of Labor was asked to examine the demands of the workplace and whether new learners are capable of meeting those demands. Specifically, the Commission was directed to advise the Secretary on the level of skills required to enter employment.

SCANS workplace competencies and foundation skills have been integrated into *HTML BASICS*. The workplace competencies are identified as 1) ability to use resources, 2) interpersonal skills, 3) ability to work with information, 4) understanding of systems, and 5) knowledge and understanding of technology. The foundation skills are identified as 1) basic communication skills, 2) thinking skills, and 3) personal qualities.

Exercises in which learners must use a number of these SCANS competencies and foundation skills are marked in the text with the SCANS icon.

How to Use This Book

What makes a good text about HTML? Sound instruction and hands-on skill-building and reinforcement. That is what you will find in *HTML BASICS*. Not only will you find a colorful and inviting layout, but also many features to enhance learning.

Objectives— Objectives are listed at the beginning of each lesson, along with a suggested time for completion of the lesson. This allows you to look ahead to what you will be learning and to pace your work.

Step-by-Step Exercises— Preceded by a short topic discussion, these exercises are the "hands-on practice" part of the lesson. Simply follow the steps to reinforce the skills and concepts you have learned.

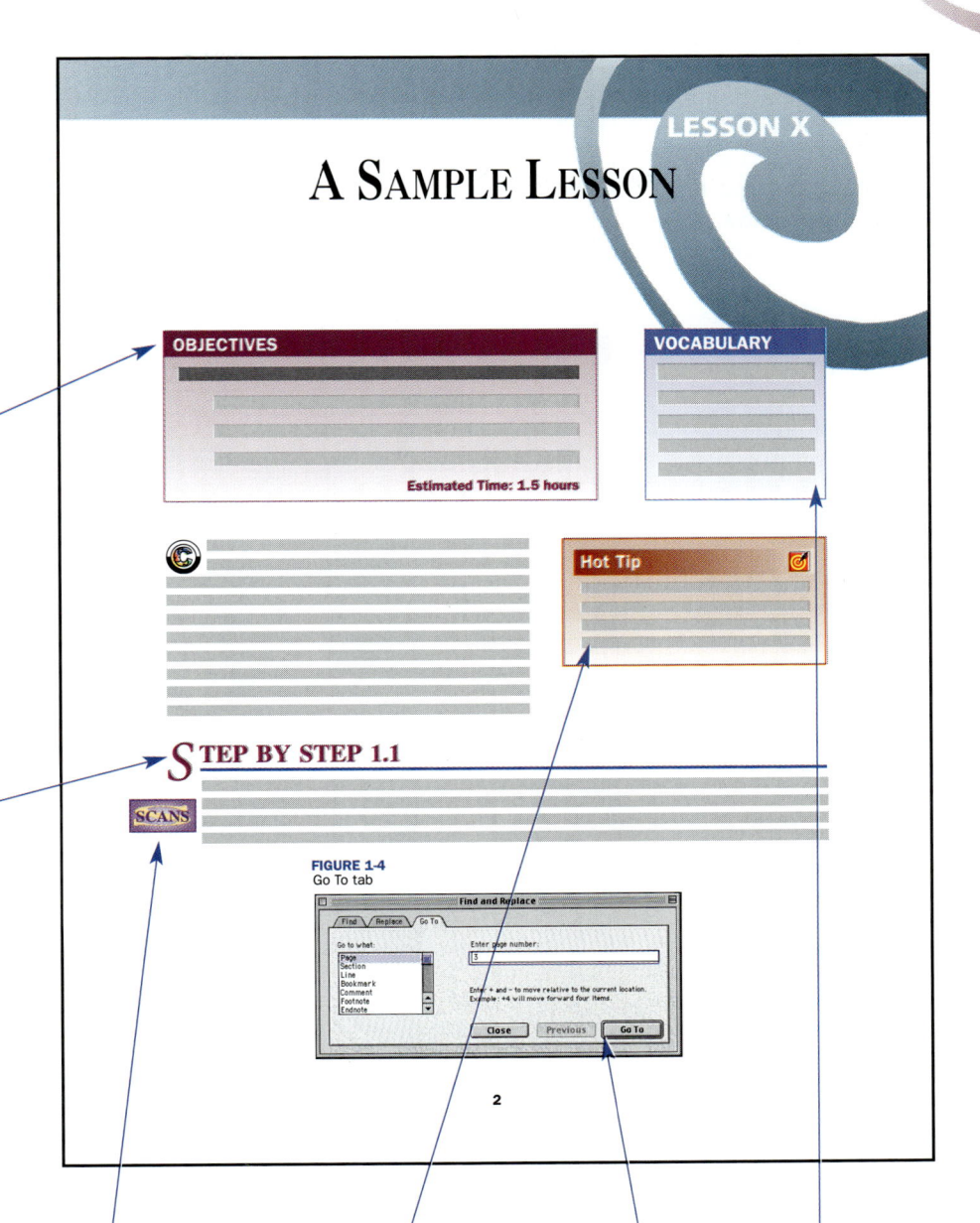

SCANS (Secretary's Commission on Achieving Necessary Skills)— The U.S. Department of Labor has identified the school-to-careers competencies.

Marginal Boxes— These boxes provide additional information about the topic of the lesson.

Vocabulary— Terms identified in boldface throughout the lesson and summarized at the end.

Enhanced Screen Shots— Screen shots now come to life on each page with color and depth.

How to Use This Book

Special Feature Boxes— These boxes provide interesting additional information about career opportunities, tips on how to create better Web pages, and historical Internet milestones.

Summary— At the end of each lesson, you will find a summary to prepare you to complete the end-of-lesson activities.

Vocabulary/Review Questions— Review material at the end of each lesson and each unit enables you to prepare for assessment of the content presented.

Lesson Projects— Hands-on application of what you have learned in the lesson allows you to apply the techniques and concepts covered.

Critical Thinking Activities— Each lesson gives you an opportunity to apply creative analysis and use the Help system to solve problems.

Command Summary— At the end of each unit, a command summary is provided for quick reference.

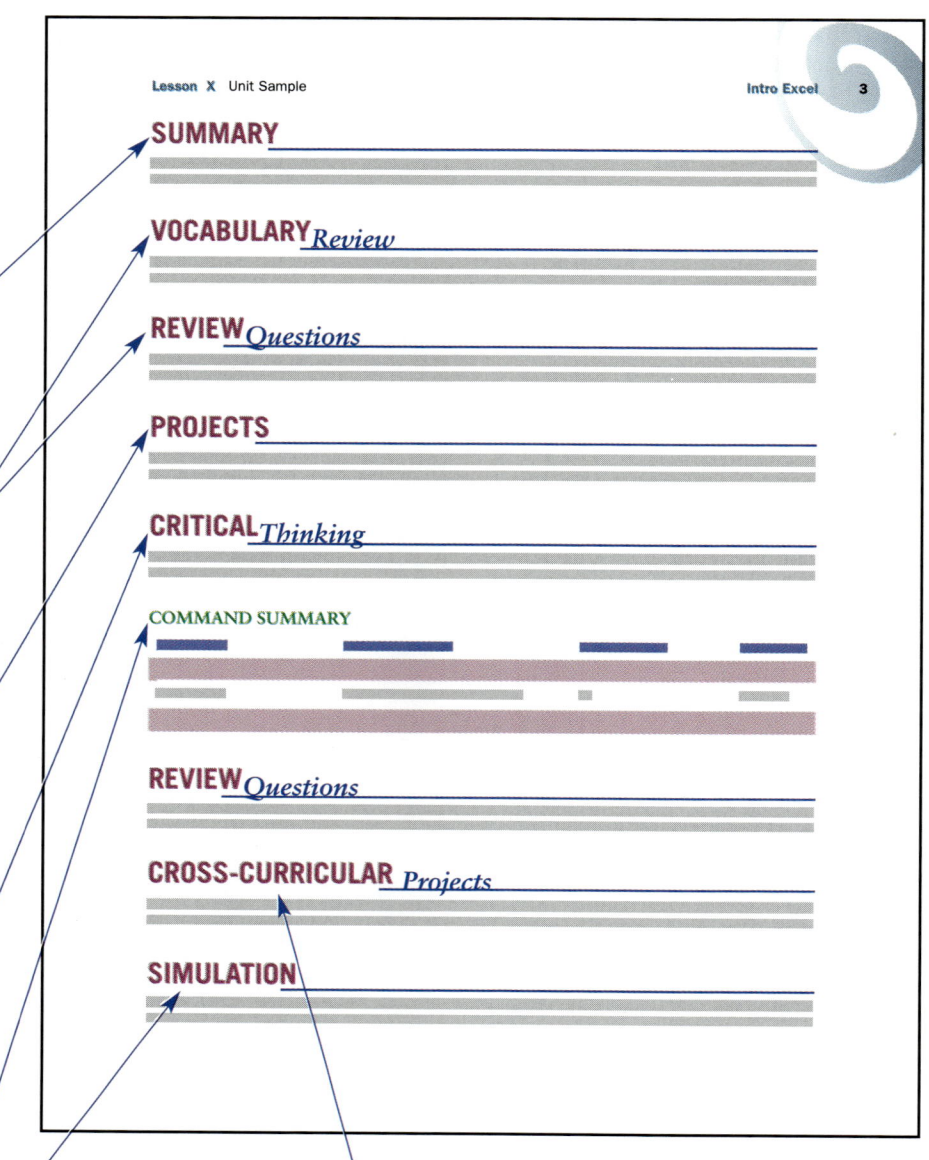

Simulation— End-of-unit hands-on jobs provide opportunity for a comprehensive review and practice for your future.

Cross-Curricular Projects— End-of-unit projects apply Internet concepts to topics across the curriculum.

HTML BASICS

Unit 1

Lesson 1 — 1.5 hrs.
Quick HTML Know-How

Lesson 2 — 1.5 hrs.
HTML Organization Techniques

Lesson 3 — 1.5 hrs.
HTML Power Techniques

Lesson 4 — 1.5 hrs.
HTML Structural Design Techniques

Estimated Time for Unit: 6 hours

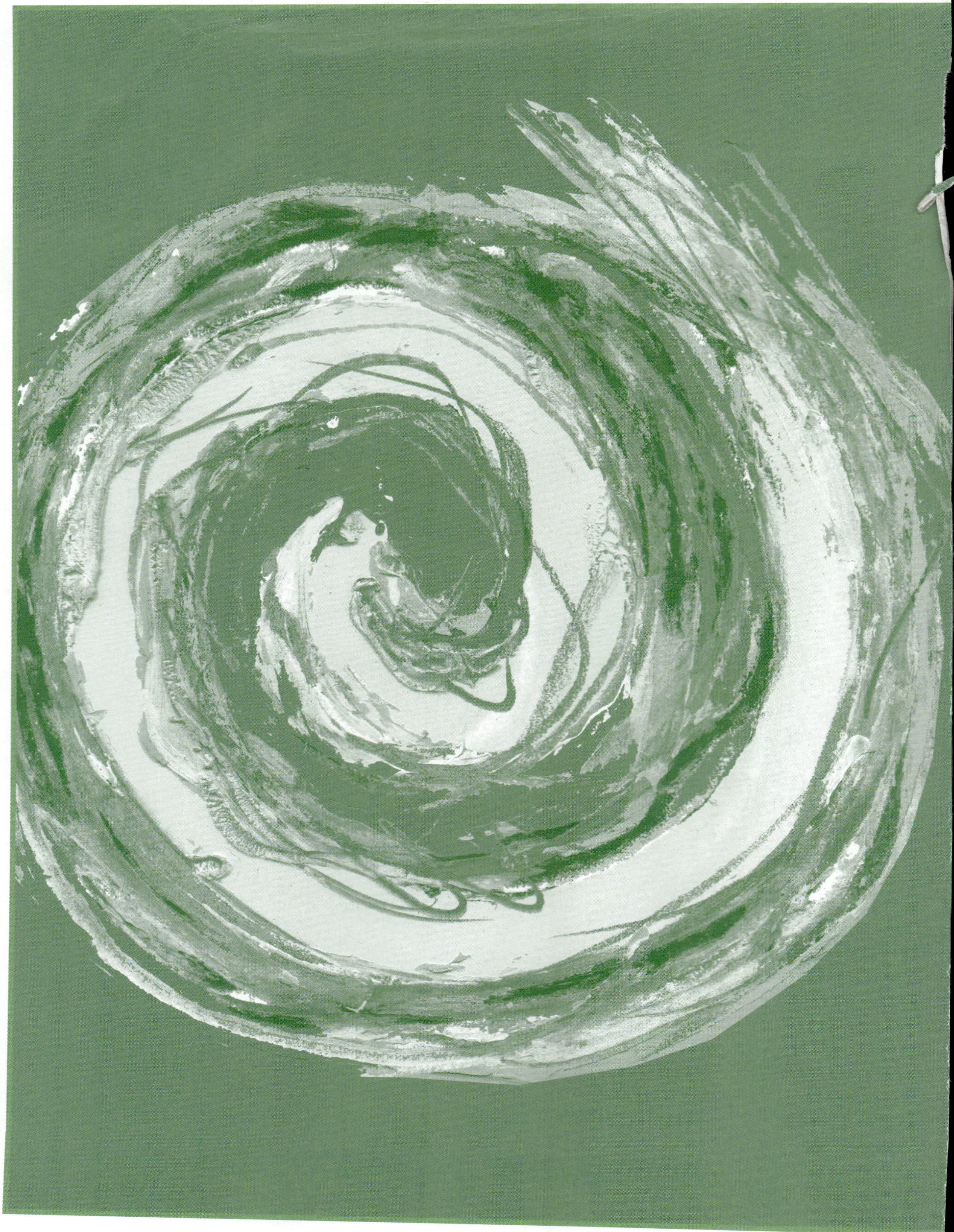

LESSON 1

QUICK HTML KNOW-HOW

OBJECTIVES

Upon completion of this lesson, you should be able to:
- Discover HTML tags.
- Enter starting tags.
- Save correctly.
- Integrate levels of headings into Web pages.
- Create unordered, ordered, and embedded lists.

Estimated Time: 1.5 hrs.

VOCABULARY

Angle brackets
Flash
Home page
HTML page
Hypertext Markup Language (HTML)
Internet Explorer
Java
JavaScript
Mosaic
Netscape Navigator
Web browser
Web page
Web site
Welcome page

Communicating on the Web

Every time you go online and begin clicking links, you'll open up one new *Web page* after another. Web pages can be composed of pictures, text, and multimedia effects. Their purpose is to share information with Web visitors. Web pages are displayed by special software programs called *Web browsers* whose job it is to find and display Web information. The two most popular browsers are *Internet Explorer* and the *Netscape Navigator*.

Hypertext Markup Language, or *HTML*, allows you to create Web pages. HTML organizes documents and tells Web browsers how Web pages should look on your computer screen. The colors, pictures, and backgrounds on Web pages are determined by HTML tags.

HTML tags work with any Web browser. If you create a Web page, and do it correctly, your Web browser can read it. In fact, HTML is the official language of the World Wide Web!

There are many other languages used in cyberspace, such as *Java*, a programming language used widely with Internet applications; *Flash*, a high impact multimedia creation tool; and *JavaScript*, a Java-like scripting language used to create miniapplications and multimedia effects. HTML is the most widely used of any of these Web page development tools. HTML creates the foundation upon which these other programs can build.

3

How HTML Works

HTML tags work everywhere on the Web. HTML tags display Web pages on Macintosh or Windows computers. They work on Linux and UNIX computers. They even work on Web-enabled cell phones, palm-sized devices, and televisions with a Web device.

HTML tags are so simple that anyone can learn a few essential tags quickly. They usually appear in pairs enclosed in *angle brackets*. These brackets can be found on the comma and period keys on your keyboard. Hold the Shift key and press either of these keys to create an angle bracket.

To more clearly understand how HTML tags work, analyze the following example. If you want to center the title of this book on a Web page, all you need to do is key:

<CENTER>HTML and JavaScript BASICS</CENTER>

Notice that there is a starting tag, **<CENTER>**, and a closing tag, **</CENTER>**. The only difference between the two tags is a slash (/) following the first angle bracket in the closing tag. **<CENTER></CENTER>** form a pair of tags, and if you haven't guessed already, these tags are called center tags. Anything between these tags will be centered on the page. Anything outside of these tags will not be affected by the command. It can't get any simpler!

Uncover the Page Beneath the Page

The Web is full of Web pages. Some are very interesting, some are very exciting, some are too busy, and some are dull and boring.

It doesn't matter if a page is interesting or dull; all pages have the same characteristics. Let's see what that means.

For example, all of the words, pictures, and colors that you see in Figure 1-1A are organized and created by the HTML tags you see in Figure 1-1B.

Figures 1-1A and 1-1B are actually the same page viewed in different ways.

FIGURE 1-1A
Course Technology home page at www.course.com

FIGURE 1-1B
HTML tags for the home page shown in Figure 1-1A

Notice that Figure 1-1B isn't very pretty. It shows the HTML tags that create the more exciting page shown in Figure 1-1A. Figure 1-1B shows exactly what the page behind the colorful page really looks like. The Web browser interprets the tags and creates the Web page that the average Web surfer sees.

There are lots of tags and lots of ways to use them. This hint should keep you from getting confused: ***The HTML tags are just instructions to the Web browser.*** They tell the browser how to display information. Many times you can look at the final Web page and guess what tags created the effect. If you remember this hint, learning HTML will be much easier.

Now it's your turn. The following steps will allow you to open a Web page of your choosing. Viewing the page behind the page is as easy as selecting Source or some similar command, such as Page Source, from the View menu in your browser (see Figures 1-3A and 1-3B).

STEP-BY-STEP 1.1

1. Open your Web browser by double-clicking its icon, as shown in Figures 1-2A and 1-2B.

FIGURE 1-2A
Internet Explorer icon

FIGURE 1-2B
Netscape Navigator icon

Lesson 1 Quick HTML Know-How · **HTML BASICS**   **7**

STEP-BY-STEP 1.1 Continued

  2. When a page appears, use your mouse to move your pointer over the View menu, as shown in Figures 1-3A and 1-3B.

FIGURE 1-3A
The View Source command in Internet Explorer

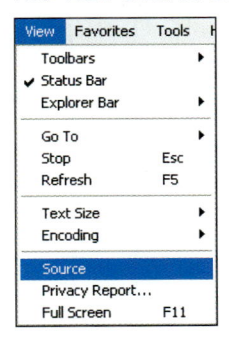

FIGURE 1-3B
The View Page Source command in Netscape Navigator

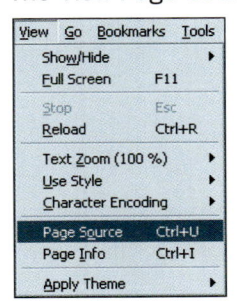

  3. Select **View** followed by **Source** in your Internet Explorer (IE) browser, or **View** followed by **Page Source** in your Netscape browser.

  4. Examine the tags that appear on the page beneath the colorful page. The tags will look something like the tags you saw in Figure 1-1B.

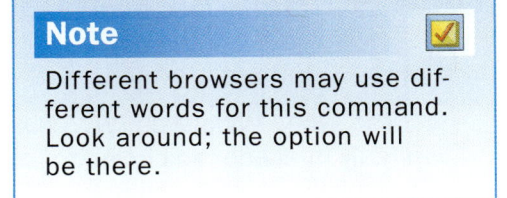

> **Note**
>
> Different browsers may use different words for this command. Look around; the option will be there.

  5. Jump around to three or four other Web pages and View the Source. List seven tags that you keep running into over and over. Guess and record what they do in the table that follows.

HTML BASICS

TABLE 1-1
Common tags

NUMBER	TAG	THE EFFECT IT CAUSES ON THE WEB
Sample	<CENTER></CENTER>	Centers text on a Web page
1		
2		
3		
4		
5		
6		
7		

6. Exit your software and shut down your computer if you are finished for today. Otherwise, continue to the next section.

Internet Milestone

Business Discovers the Web

The World Wide Web (WWW) was created in the late 1980s in Europe. It was used limitedly in academic circles for about the next five years. However, it didn't capture the public's imagination until 1994 when a Web browser called **Mosaic** came on the scene. It was the first Web browser that allowed both pictures and text to accompany Web pages.

Excitement grew around this new way to present and share information. Then, Netscape Communications Corp. released its browser called Netscape Navigator. Netscape caught the imagination of businesses in 1995, and everything was different from that point on.

In just a few short years, the World Wide Web became the new advertising and commercial medium that we see today. Billions and billions of dollars were invested by companies and corporations hoping to cash in on this new golden information-sharing system. Suddenly, thousands and thousands of corporate Web page creators began to learn HTML so they could put their business Web pages online.

Enter Your Mystery Tags the Old-Fashioned Way

Before you start entering tags, you need to be aware of the many terms used to describe pages created with HTML tags. The truth is, these names are used so interchangeably that most people are totally unaware that there are slight distinctions in their meanings.

- *Web page*: Also referred to as a Web document, any page created in HTML that can be placed on the World Wide Web.
- *Home page*: The main or primary Web page for a corporation, organization, or for an individual. A personal home page is the first page you see as you start up your Web browser. When you click the Home icon in the browser, you will go directly to your starting home page.
- *Welcome page*: Designed especially for new visitors to a site.
- *HTML page*: Also referred to as an HTML document, any document created in HTML that can be displayed on the World Wide Web.
- *Web site*: Can include a collection of many interconnected Web pages organized by a specific company, organization, college or university, government agency, or individual. Web sites are stored on Web servers. There are many Web sites and thousands of HTML pages on each Web site.

Is it all clear now? Don't let these subtle distinctions get in the way of your understanding of how the Web works.

Creating a Powerful Advantage with Tags

There are many ways to create HTML tags. You can use specialized software, such as FrontPage by Microsoft, GoLive from Adobe, or Dreamweaver from Macromedia, to create super Web pages. These programs help organize your HTML page, enter text, move things around, and create superior Web page effects without ever entering an HTML tag. You can do the same with many of the newer versions of word processing programs, such as Microsoft Word and Corel WordPerfect. These word processors have built-in HTML tags.

You will want to use one of these programs for most of your Web pages. For the following activity, however, you are going to enter HTML tags the old-fashioned way. Learning to enter a few HTML tags in the old-fashioned way will give you a big advantage as you start to learn JavaScript in Unit 2. Let's quickly cover the basics. First, by entering a few tags, you will develop a deeper understanding of how HTML really works. Second, you'll be able to troubleshoot Web pages when picky little errors occur. Third, you'll be able to view other pages and learn how they achieve certain effects. Fourth, you'll understand a little better the file and folder structures found on Web computers. Finally, and most importantly, you'll understand how HTML and JavaScript work together.

What to Use

Almost any word processing program or text editor will work for creating both HTML and JavaScript. This is one of the reasons HTML and JavaScript are so popular. You do not need any specialized software tools in order to create exciting Web pages like you need for Java, Shockwave, or some of the other software-intensive options.

Our recommendation is to use the simplest, most basic tools available. In Windows, you can use Notepad. On a Macintosh, you can use SimpleText. These programs are easy to use and available on nearly every computer on the planet. Use your favorite word processing program, such as Microsoft Word, Corel WordPerfect, or AppleWorks. However, you will need to experiment a little bit with each word processing program to learn its idiosyncrasies. Instructions for Microsoft Word and AppleWorks are provided in this text as examples. Many other word processors have similar HTML creation features. Check the software's help system if you have any difficulties, or revert to Notepad or SimpleText to complete the Step-by-Step activities.

> **Net Tip**
>
> Sophisticated software programs, such as Dreamweaver, GoLive, and FrontPage, really streamline the job of creating classy Web pages quickly. These programs provide options that allow you to see the tags. If you're using one of these programs, select the HTML Source option so you can enter the tags directly.

STEP-BY-STEP 1.2

1. Open Notepad, SimpleText, or your favorite word processing software.

2. Create a new document if necessary.

3. Enter the tags shown in Figure 1-4 in this exact order. Don't leave out any angle bracket (<) or slash (/). Everything is important.

FIGURE 1-4
Enter these tags exactly as shown here

```
<HTML>
<TITLE></TITLE>
<BODY>
<CENTER></CENTER>
<P></P>
<P></P>
<P></P>
<P></P>
<P></P>
</BODY>
</HTML>
```

STEP-BY-STEP 1.2 Continued

4. The tags you just entered are called the basic tags. They include a standard set of tags that appear in most Web pages. But your page will look very sad without some text. Enter the text between the tags, as shown in Figure 1-5. Notice that the new text to be entered is shown in bold.

FIGURE 1-5
Enter the text between the tags exactly as shown here

```
<HTML>
<TITLE>HTML and JavaScript</TITLE>
<BODY>
<CENTER>Creating HTML and JavaScript</CENTER>
<P>Learning to create HTML tags can help you in many ways:</P>
<P>You will develop a deeper understanding of how HTML really works.</P>
<P>You will be able to troubleshoot Web pages when errors occur.</P>
<P>You will be able to view other pages and learn how certain effects were created.</P>
<P>You will understand how HTML and JavaScript work together.</P>
</BODY>
</HTML>
```

5. Leave your text editor open and go on to Step-by-Step 1.3, where you will learn how to save HTML files.

Save and View Your HTML Page

HTML documents are text files. This means that they are saved in the simplest way possible. For the most part, text files only save the letters you see on your keyboard. All of the sophisticated word processing commands are erased, leaving just the letters.

Saving as text allows HTML files to move quickly over the Web. However, the problem with text files is that most people don't know how to save them. Before you save, there are a few things you need to know first.

To tell one kind of file from another, computers often add file extensions to filenames. Sometimes you can see these extensions on your computer and sometimes you can't. Depending on your computer's settings, the extensions may or may not be visible, but the software on your computer knows the kinds of file types it can open.

Net Tip

HTML isn't case sensitive. You can use uppercase <TAGS>, or you can use lowercase <tags>. Uppercase <TAGS> are easier to see. If you're emphasizing the tags, use uppercase <TAGS>. If you would rather emphasize the words in the document, use lowercase <tags>.

You can even mix uppercase <TAGS> and lowercase <tags> together like <Tag> or <TAG></tag>. However, mixing cases is not considered good form.

Extensions are used a lot. For example, in Windows, text files are saved with a .txt ending or extension. If you use a word processor much, you may have seen these popular extensions:

.doc   Microsoft Word document
.rtf   Microsoft's Rich Text Format
.wpd   Corel WordPerfect document

12 HTML BASICS

.txt   text file
.html   HTML file
.htm   HTML file on some computer systems

HTML files are text files with an .html or .htm extension. While the format that you need for HTML is called text, the ending or extension must be .html (or .htm if you're using older Windows-based software programs). The .html or .htm extensions signal to the Web browser that this is an HTML text file. The .html extension is like putting up a sign saying, "Hey, browser, read me. I'm an HTML document."

Follow along. We are going to show you how to save with different software programs. Use the software instructions that most closely resemble the software on your computer system. They are Notepad, Microsoft Word, SimpleText, and AppleWorks.

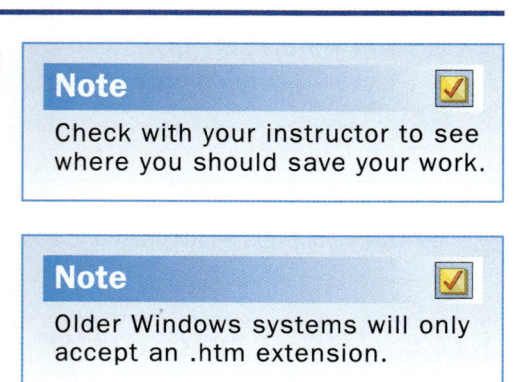

STEP-BY-STEP 1.3

1. Select **Save As** from the **File** menu. (Microsoft Word users beware! DO NOT select Save as Web page from the File menu! Use the regular Save As command.)

   > **Note**
   > Check with your instructor to see where you should save your work.

2. From the Save As dialog box, create a new folder in which to save your HTML and JavaScript work.

3. For both Notepad in Windows and SimpleText for Macintosh, the steps are very similar. Word and AppleWorks users should skip to Step 5.

   > **Note**
   > Older Windows systems will only accept an .htm extension.

4. Select the folder into which you wish to save your files.

5. Name your file one.html as shown in Figure 1-6. Check with your instructor to make sure you save your file properly. Click Save. If everything saved okay, go on to Step 6.

FIGURE 1-6
Name a text file with an .html extension

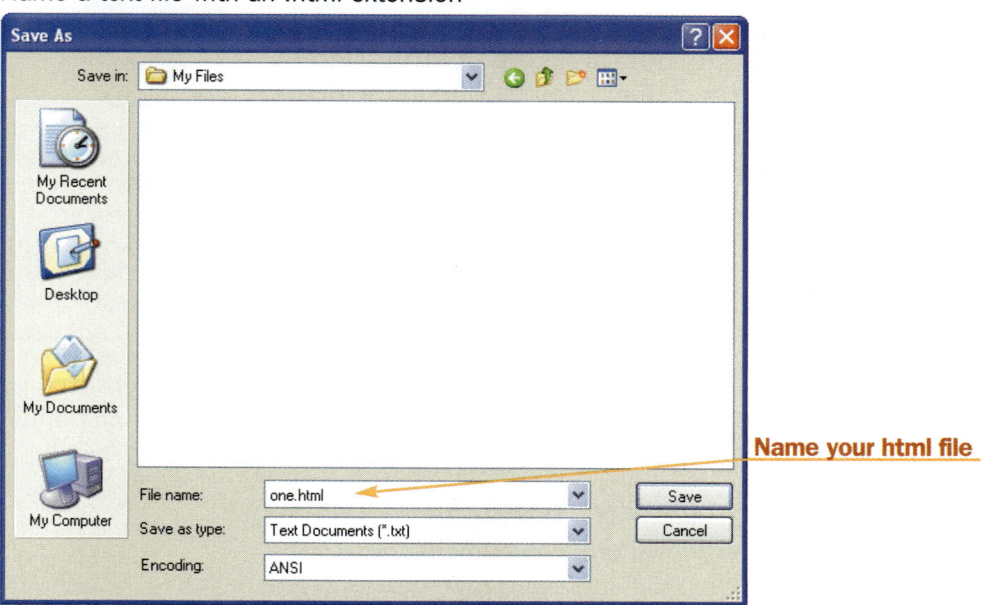

Lesson 1 Quick HTML Know-How   **HTML BASICS** 13

STEP-BY-STEP 1.3 Continued

In your word processing software, there are a few additional steps. While Notepad and SimpleText automatically save as text only, word processors save in their own unique format. You must select the proper text format from your saving options. Instructions for Word and AppleWorks are provided here to help you to learn this important step. Other word processors may have their own text saving options. Check with your instructor to make sure you are following the steps properly for your software.

If you are a **Microsoft Word** user, perform the following steps.

a. Locate the folder in which you want to place your file.

b. Select **Plain Text** as the **Save as type** or format type, as shown in Figure 1-7.

c. Name your file **one.html**.

d. Choose **Save**.

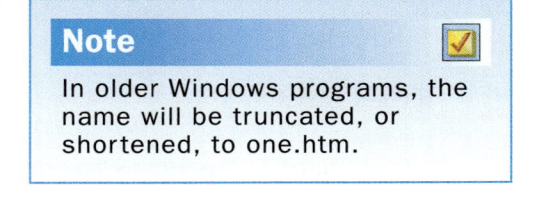

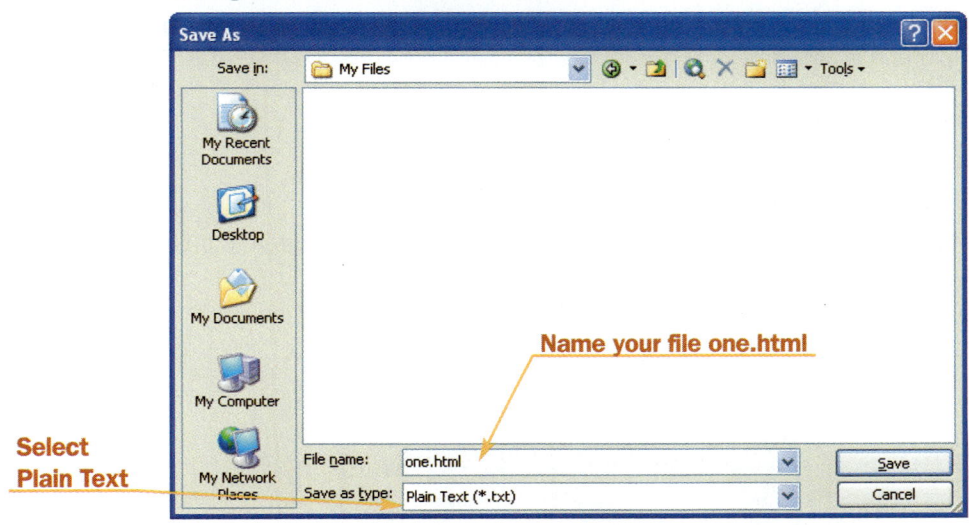

Note

In older Windows programs, the name will be truncated, or shortened, to one.htm.

FIGURE 1-7
Saving text files in Microsoft Word

If you are an **AppleWorks** user, perform the following steps.

a. Locate the folder into which you want to place your file.

b. Select **Plain Text** as the **File Format**.

14 HTML BASICS

HTML Basics Unit

STEP-BY-STEP 1.3 Continued

  c. Name your file **one.html**, as shown in Figure 1-8.
  d. Choose **Save**.

FIGURE 1-8
Saving text files in AppleWorks

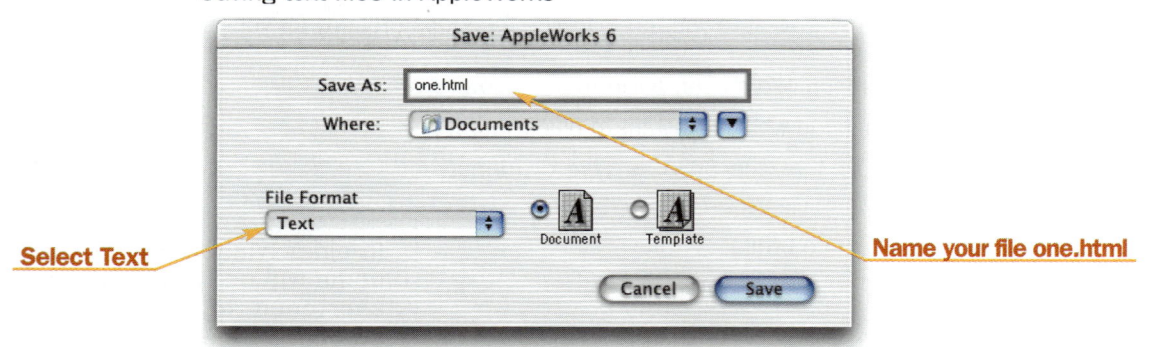

Select Text — File Format: Text

Name your file one.html — Save As: one.html

6. Viewing your HTML page in a Web browser is easy. We'll show you how to do this in Netscape and Internet Explorer.

   If you are an **Internet Explorer** user, perform the following steps.
   a. Open your Web browser.
   b. Select **File**, and then **Open**.
   c. Locate the folder where you saved your file. Choose the **Browse** button to do this.
   d. Select your HTML file in the Open text box, and choose **Open**.
   e. Click **OK**, as shown in Figure 1-9.

FIGURE 1-9
Find your file in IE

Click OK

   If you are a **Netscape Navigator** user, perform the following steps.
   a. Open your Web browser.
   b. From the **File** menu, choose **Open File**.
   c. Select **All files** under the Files of type option, if necessary.

Lesson 1 Quick HTML Know-How

HTML BASICS 15

STEP-BY-STEP 1.3 Continued

   d. Browse to the folder where you saved your file.

   e. Select your HTML file, and click **Open** as shown in Figure 1-10.

FIGURE 1-10
Find your file in Netscape

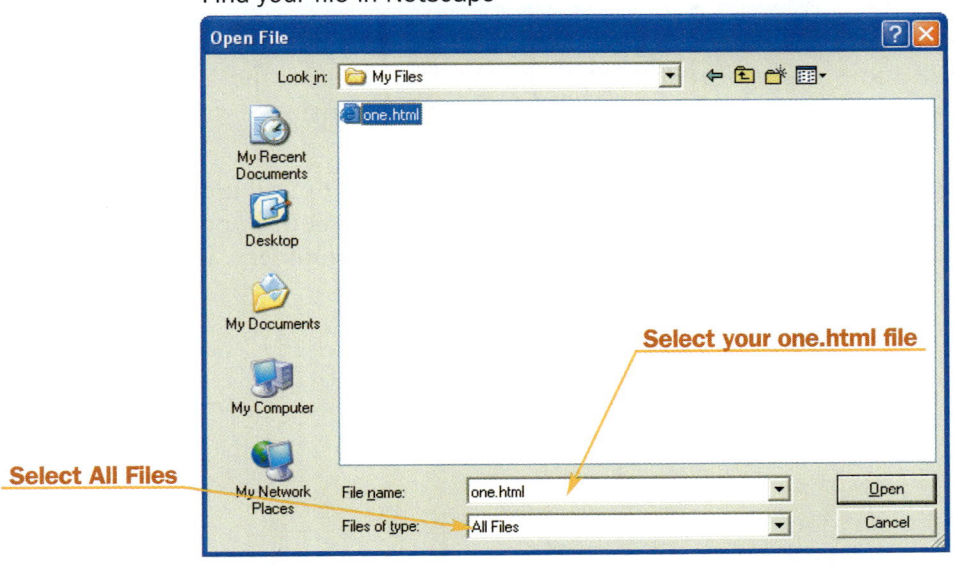

7. View your file. It should look like Figure 1-11.

FIGURE 1-11
Congratulations! Your Web page probably looks like this sample!

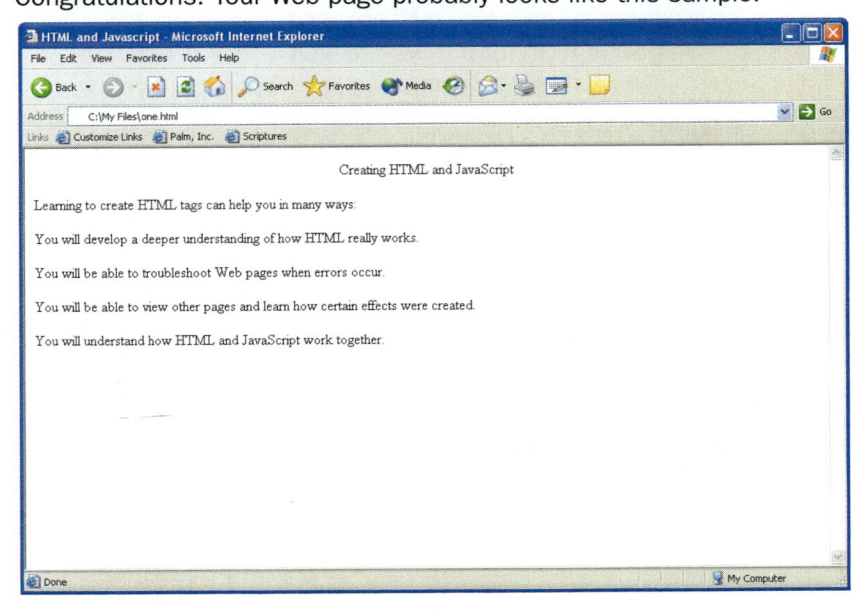

8. How does your Web page look? Make any corrections necessary, save again, return to your browser, and then click **Reload** or **Refresh** to see the changes you have made.

Using Headings

Most printed documents use headings to help the reader find important portions of text. Think of a report you have written for school. The main heading usually appears at the top and in the center of the page. Subheadings or secondary headings usually appear at the side of the paper. They are often shown in bold.

HTML gives you six standard headings, or title sizes, from which to choose. In later Step-by-Steps, you'll learn of more sophisticated ways to manipulate the size and appearance of text. Nevertheless, the heading tags provide an easy way to control the size of your text, making it stand out so your reader can view the headings clearly.

The heading tags are easy to remember. They use the letter H with a number from 1 to 6 to indicate the level of the heading. Heading numbers indicate the level of importance for marked headings, with 1 being the most prominent and 6 being the least prominent. Look for:

<H1></H1>

<H2></H2>

<H3></H3>

<H4></H4>

<H5></H5>

<H6></H6>

Internet Milestone

The Browser Wars

In the last few years, Netscape and Internet Explorer have been fighting it out for supremacy in the Web browser world. But this wasn't the first browser battle. In 1994, the dominant browser was called Mosaic. It was freeware out of the National Supercomputing Center at the University of Illinois in Champaign-Urbana. At the time Netscape came on the scene, Mosaic was adding 600,000 new users a month. But things changed in a hurry.

In the first three months of 1995, Netscape's Navigator browser gained a reputation for being a faster browser. By midyear it had captured 50% of browser users, and by the end of the year it commanded a whopping 80% of the browser market.

Netscape's dominance was quickly challenged by rival Microsoft, which came out with its Internet Explorer browser. Microsoft gave away copies of its browser in hopes of cutting into Netscape's lead. Microsoft also had an advantage in that its Windows operating system ran on over 90% of personal computers. By making Windows and Internet Explorer work together, Microsoft created a more user-friendly Web system.

Microsoft's advantage, however, lead to many legal battles. Several antitrust lawsuits argued that Microsoft was using its dominance in Windows to crush Netscape and to eliminate its competition unfairly. Microsoft claimed it was simply adding more value for its customers by making its Internet Explorer browser easier to access.

The browser wars continue today. Although Microsoft's Internet Explorer is still the dominant player in most markets, Netscape's Navigator is still very popular in many circles. In addition, there are other new Web browsers that are making their move into cyberspace. These browsers include Firefox, Camino, Opera, and Safari. Who will win in the end?

Lesson 1 Quick HTML Know-How

HTML BASICS 17

Anything inside the heading tags will be made larger or smaller, depending on the number. For example:

<H1>VERY BIG</H1>

<H3>In the Middle</H3>

<H6>Very Small</H6>

In this Step-by-Step, you will open the HTML file you have been working on and add the heading or title tags.

STEP-BY-STEP 1.4

1. Open your text editor.

2. Open your **one.html** or **one.htm** file, if necessary. If you are using Notepad, select **All Files** under the **Files of type** option, as shown in Figure 1-12A. Otherwise, you will not be able to view your .html or .htm file! If you are using Microsoft Word, when you open an .html file, Word may display your Web page as it would appear in a Web browser. In order to view the HTML tags, select **HTML Source** from the **View** menu, as shown in Figure 1-12B.

> **Hot Tip**
>
> When you select HTML Source on the View menu in Word, a dialog box may appear stating that the HTML Source Editor feature is not yet installed. You may need to insert the Office CD and install this feature before you can view the HTML source.

FIGURE 1-12A
Notepad users

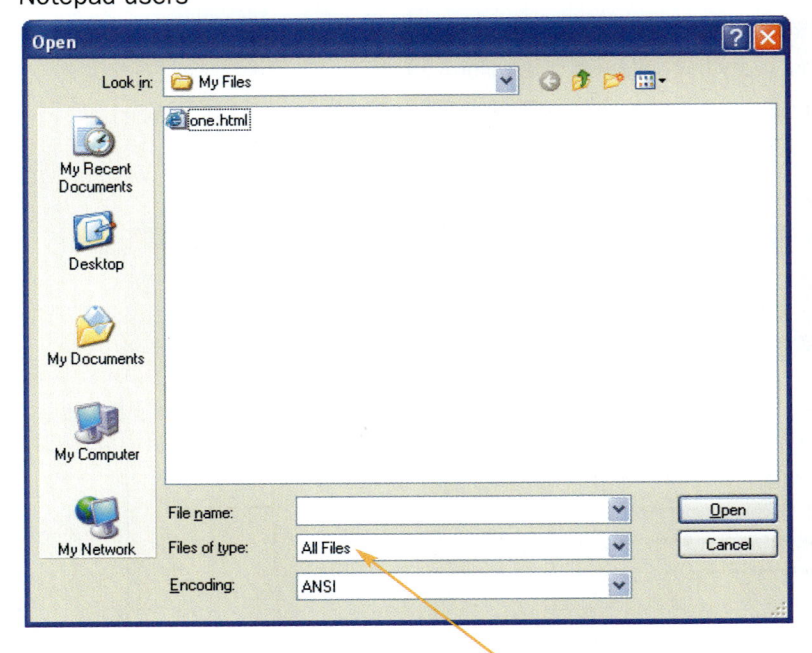

FIGURE 1-12B
MS Word users

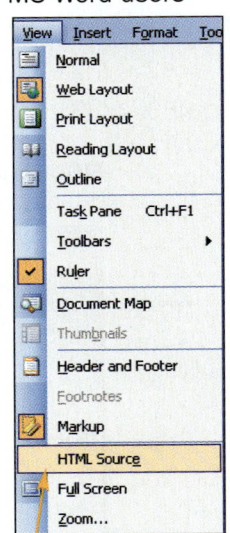

Select All Files

Select HTML Source

STEP-BY-STEP 1.4 Continued

3. Enter the heading tags shown in bold in Figure 1-13.

FIGURE 1-13
Add the heading tags

```
<HTML>
<TITLE>HTML and JavaScript</TITLE>
<BODY>
<CENTER><H1>Creating HTML and JavaScript</H1></CENTER>
<P><H2>Learning to create HTML tags can help you in many ways: </H2></P>
<P><H3>You will develop a deeper understanding of how HTML really works. </H3></P>
<P><H4>You will be able to troubleshoot Web pages when errors occur. </H4></P>
<P><H5>You will be able to view other pages and learn how certain effects were created.
</H5></P>
<P><H6>You will understand how HTML and JavaScript work together. </H6></P>
</BODY>
</HTML>
```

4. Save your new HTML page as **two.html** or **two.htm**.

5. Open your Web browser. Open your **two.html** or **two.htm** file, and view it. It should look like Figure 1-14. (Navigator users may see the "Pop-Up Block" option turned On and Off. Simply click the button to toggle the current setting.) Heading tags really change the look of a page. In our example in Figure 1-14, however, the heading tags are misused. At best, there are only three levels of information:

   <H1></H1> The title at the top

   <H2></H2> The introductory line followed by a colon (:)

   <H3></H3> The list of the reasons to learn HTML tags

FIGURE 1-14
Headings in a Web page

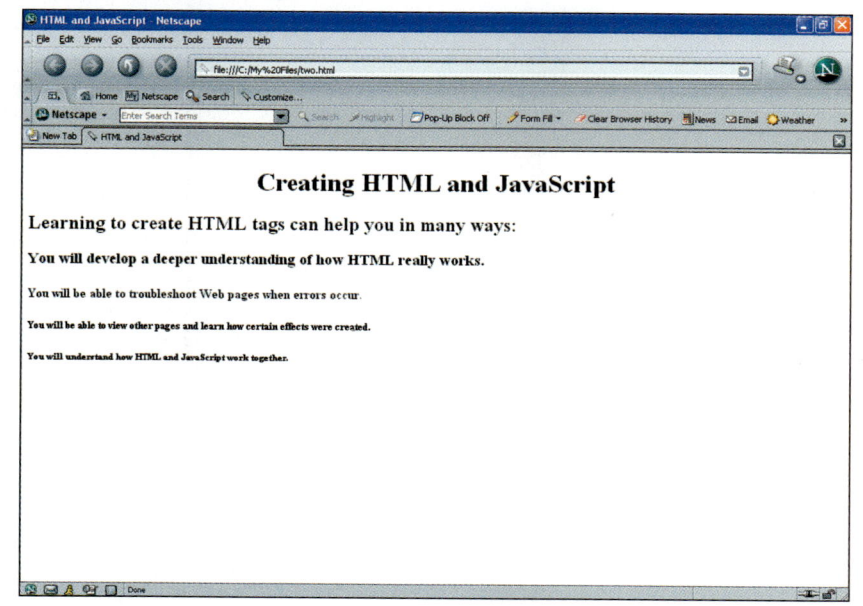

Lesson 1 Quick HTML Know-How

HTML BASICS

STEP-BY-STEP 1.4 Continued

6. Return to your document and reorganize the heading tags. Use no more than three <H></H> tags. Think about your tag choices for a second, then make your document comfortable to read, emphasizing the three levels this document dictates. Resave your file to make your changes become effective.

7. Exit your software and shut down your computer if you are finished for today. Otherwise, continue to the next section.

Numbered and Bulleted Lists

In the last Step-by-Step, you were asked to reorganize your two.html file and use the <H> tags in a more consistent manner. In this Step-by-Step, we are going to whip things into shape even further.

One of the most powerful ways to organize information on a Web page is by the use of lists. There are several kinds of lists, including the following:

Unordered (or Bulleted) lists	<UL></UL>
Ordered (or Numbered) lists	<OL></OL>

The unordered lists tags <UL></UL> create bulleted lists. Start your list with the opening <UL> unordered lists tag, mark the items to be listed with the list <LI></LI> tags, and place an </UL> tag at the end of your list. Try it!

STEP-BY-STEP 1.5

1. Open your **two.html** or **two.htm** file for text editing.

STEP-BY-STEP 1.5 Continued

2. Enter the **<UL></UL>** tags at the start and at the end of the list to create an unordered list, as shown in Figure 1-15.

FIGURE 1-15
Enter the unordered list tags

```
<HTML>
<TITLE>HTML and JavaScript</TITLE>
<BODY>
<CENTER><H1>Creating HTML and JavaScript</H1></CENTER>
<P><H2>Learning to create HTML tags can help you in many ways: </H2></P>

<UL>
<LI><H3>You will develop a deeper understanding of how HTML really works. </H3></LI>
<LI><H3>You will be able to troubleshoot Web pages when errors occur. </H3></LI>
<LI><H3>You will be able to view other pages and learn how certain effects were created. </H3></LI>
<LI><H3>You will understand how HTML and JavaScript work together. </H3></LI>
</UL>

</BODY>
</HTML>
```

3. Replace the **<P>** and **</P>** tags with **<LI>** and **</LI>** tags for each sentence in the list, as shown in Figure 1-15.

4. Save your file as **three.html** or **three.htm**.

Lesson 1 Quick HTML Know-How

HTML BASICS

STEP-BY-STEP 1.5 Continued

5. View your page in a browser to see how it looks. It should be similar to Figure 1-16.

FIGURE 1-16
An unordered list

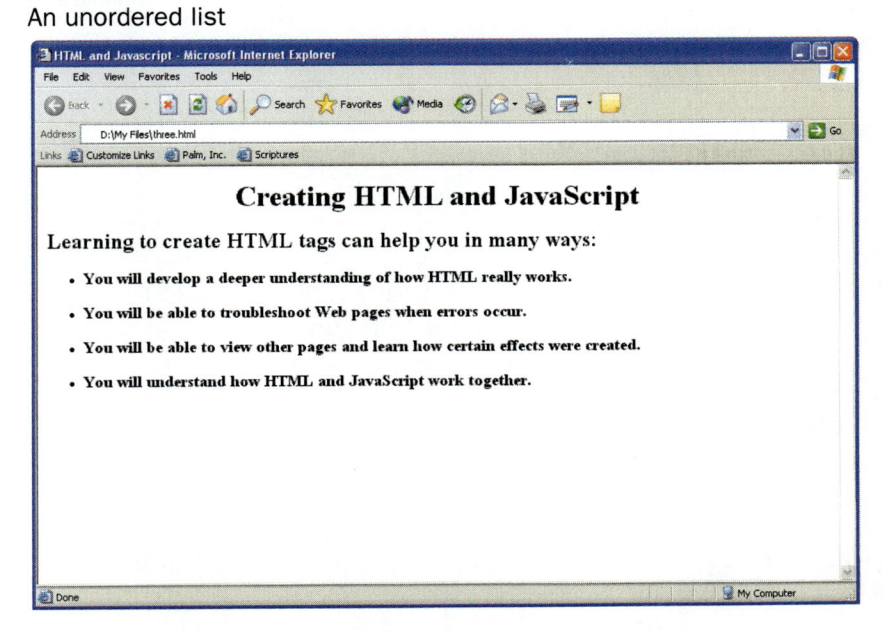

6. Open your **three.html** or **three.htm** file for text editing, if necessary.

STEP-BY-STEP 1.5 Continued

7. Change the pair of **<UL></UL>** tags to **<OL></OL>** tags to change your list from an unordered list to an ordered list, as shown in Figure 1-17. No other changes are necessary.

> **Note**
> Don't use a zero; use the letter O for ordered.

FIGURE 1-17
Enter the ordered lists tags

```
<HTML>
<TITLE>HTML and JavaScript</TITLE>
<BODY>
<CENTER><H1>Creating HTML and JavaScript</H1></CENTER>
<P><H2>Learning to create HTML tags can help you in many ways: </H2></P>

<OL>
<LI><H3>You will develop a deeper understanding of how HTML really works.
</H3></LI>
<LI><H3>You will be able to troubleshoot Web pages when errors occur.
</H3></LI>
<LI><H3>You will be able to view other pages and learn how certain effects were created.
</H3></LI>
<LI><H3>You will understand how HTML and JavaScript work together.
</H3></LI>
</OL>

</BODY>
</HTML>
```

8. Save your file as **four.html** or **four.htm**.

Lesson 1 Quick HTML Know-How

HTML BASICS 23

STEP-BY-STEP 1.5 Continued

9. View your page in a browser to see how it looks. It should look similar to Figure 1-18.

FIGURE 1-18
An ordered or numbered list

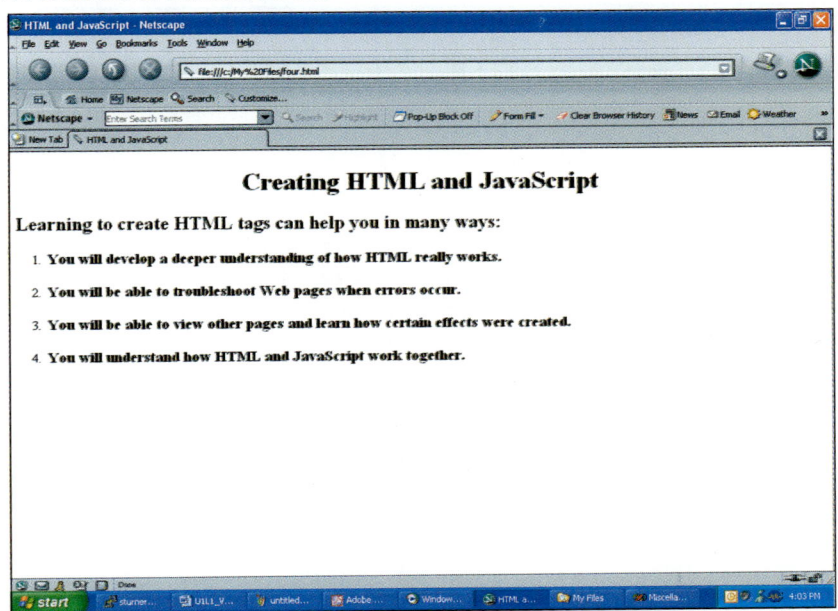

10. Open your **four.html** or **four.htm** file for text editing, if necessary.

STEP-BY-STEP 1.5 Continued

11. Add two pairs of **<UL></UL>** tags in the middle of the list, as shown in Figure 1-19.

FIGURE 1-19
Enter the unordered lists tags

```
<HTML>
<TITLE>HTML and JavaScript</TITLE>
<BODY>
<CENTER><H1>Creating HTML and JavaScript</H1></CENTER>
<P><H2>Learning to create HTML tags can help you in many ways: </H2></P>

<OL>
<LI><H3>You will develop a deeper understanding of how HTML really works.
</H3></LI>

<UL>
<LI><H3>You will be able to troubleshoot Web pages when errors occur. </H3></LI>
<UL>
<LI><H3>You will be able to view other pages and learn how certain effects were created.
</H3></LI>
</UL>
</UL>

<LI><H3>You will understand how HTML and JavaScript work together.
</H3></LI>
</OL>
</BODY>
</HTML>
```

12. Save your file as **five.html** or **five.htm**.

Lesson 1 Quick HTML Know-How

HTML BASICS 25

STEP-BY-STEP 1.5 Continued

13. View your page to see how it looks. It should look similar to Figure 1-20.

FIGURE 1-20
Embedded and indented lists

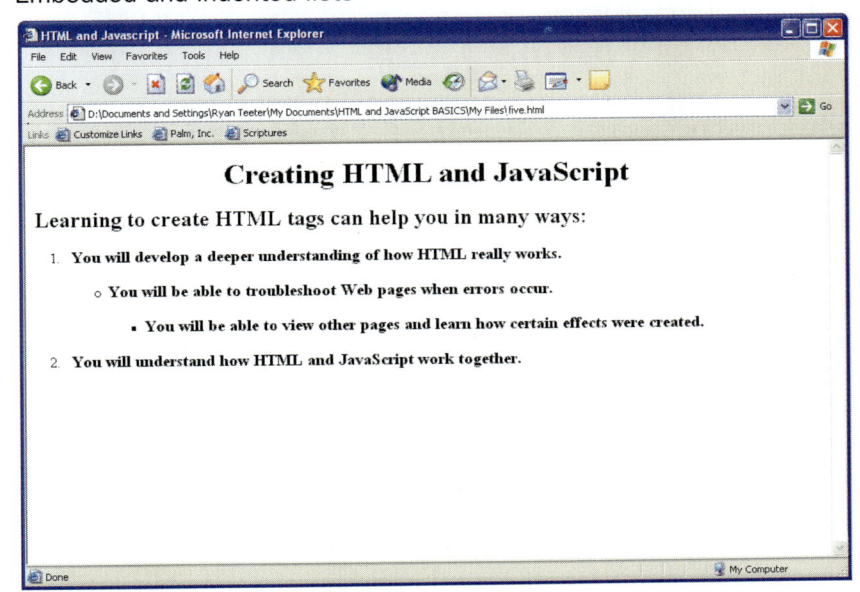

14. Exit your software and shut down your computer if you are finished for today. Otherwise, continue to the Summary section.

SUMMARY

In this lesson, you learned:
- You can identify HTML tags.
- You can enter your starting tags.
- You can save your HTML file correctly.
- You can integrate levels of headings into Web pages.
- You can create unordered, ordered, and embedded lists.

HTML BASICS

VOCABULARY Review

Define the following terms:

Angle brackets	Internet Explorer	Web browser
Flash	Java	Web page
Home page	JavaScript	Web site
HTML page	Mosaic	Welcome page
Hypertext Markup Language (HTML)	Netscape Navigator	

REVIEW Questions

TRUE/FALSE

Circle T if the statement is true or F if the statement is false.

T   F   1. The <LI> tag defines a list item.

T   F   2. The <OL> tag creates a bulleted list.

T   F   3. The <CENTER> tag formats text so that it is centered on the page.

T   F   4. Learning HTML is very difficult.

T   F   5. The <UL> tag creates a list with no particular order.

FILL IN THE BLANK

Complete the following sentences by writing the correct word or words in the blanks provided.

1. An unordered or _____ list shows items in no particular order.

2. An ordered or _____ list shows items in a numerical order.

3. File _____ are three-letter suffixes that tell what type of file a file is.

4. _____ was the first Web browser that Netscape competed against.

5. HTML is made up of _____, which are commands enclosed in angle brackets (< >).

Lesson 1 Quick HTML Know-How

WRITTEN QUESTIONS

Write a short answer to each of the following questions:

1. Think of a way to explain how HTML tags work to people who have never created a Web page before in their lives. How can you explain how HTML works to a novice?

2. Explain the process of viewing the HTML source code for an HTML Web page.

3. Explain how you must save HTML text pages.

4. What are filename extensions? Give examples.

5. What are Mosaic, Netscape Navigator, and Internet Explorer? What has each contributed to the growth of the Web?

PROJECTS

PROJECT 1-1

You have just been hired as the Webmaster for GreatApplications, Inc., a major software and Web site developer, but your HTML skills are limited. You need to find some good HTML information fast! What do you do?

HTML BASICS

The answer is obvious. Hit the Web. Pick a search portal, such as Yahoo!, Excite, Lycos, or some other search site, and enter the search words:

Hypertext Markup Language
HTML
HTML Guides
Learning HTML

Use the following table to record the titles and URLs or Web addresses and write a brief summary of the helpful HTML Web pages you find:

TABLE 1-2
Helpful Web pages

TITLE THAT APPEARS IN THE TITLE BAR	WEB ADDRESS OR URL	DESCRIPTION

TEAMWORK PROJECT

GreatApplications, Inc. is looking for design ideas for their new Web site welcome page. In a team of three or four, create a list of your favorite Web pages. Find seven great Web pages and discuss what makes them so cool. Vote, and make your vote count as you rank the seven welcome pages from Number 1 to Number 7. List your team's choices below for future reference.

TABLE 1-3
Well-designed Web pages

RANKING	TITLE AS IT APPEARS IN THE TITLE BAR	WEB ADDRESS OR URL
1.		
2.		
3.		
4.		
5.		
6.		
7.		

WEB PROJECT

Web sites are important for many companies, groups, and individuals. We all know that many corporations would go out of business without their quality Web sites. But just how important are great-looking Web sites for noncommercial organizations and government agencies?

List reasons why these organizations need Web sites:

Government agencies:

Nonprofit organizations:

Universities:

CRITICAL *Thinking*

Prepare a 100- to 250-word answer to each of the following questions.

SCANS ACTIVITY 1-1

The World Wide Web is a large web of computer networks that share HTML files. You can visit a new Web page every minute of every day for the rest of your life and never come close to reading a fraction of the available Web pages. How many millions or billions of Web pages exist in cyberspace? While HTML has allowed people to share Web pages easily, has HTML also contributed to information overload? If so, how?

SCANS ACTIVITY 1-2

There is an error in the following set of tags and you are to find it and fix it. What will the current tags do to your page? What does it look like after you make the correction?

<OL>
<LI>Item A</LI>
<UL>
<LI>Item A1</LI>
<LI>Item A2</LI>
</UL>
<LI>Item B</LI>
<UL>
<LI>Item B1</LI>
<LI>Item B2</LI>
</UL>
</UL>

SCANS ACTIVITY 1-3

How can you create a sophisticated outline in HTML (you know, the kind you had to do for your last research paper)? In what ways can your research paper be enhanced online in HTML?

SUMMARY *Project*

All good authors know that before starting a big writing project it is often a good idea to create an outline of the information they wish to present. Outlines can be very effective in helping writers organize their thoughts, and to make sure their writing follows a logical flow of ideas. Use the HTML skills you have learned in this lesson to create an outline for a book which is composed of units, chapters, and sections. Figure 1-21 below will give you an idea of how your completed outline should look.

Lesson 1 Quick HTML Know-How

HTML BASICS

FIGURE 1-21
A sample book outline

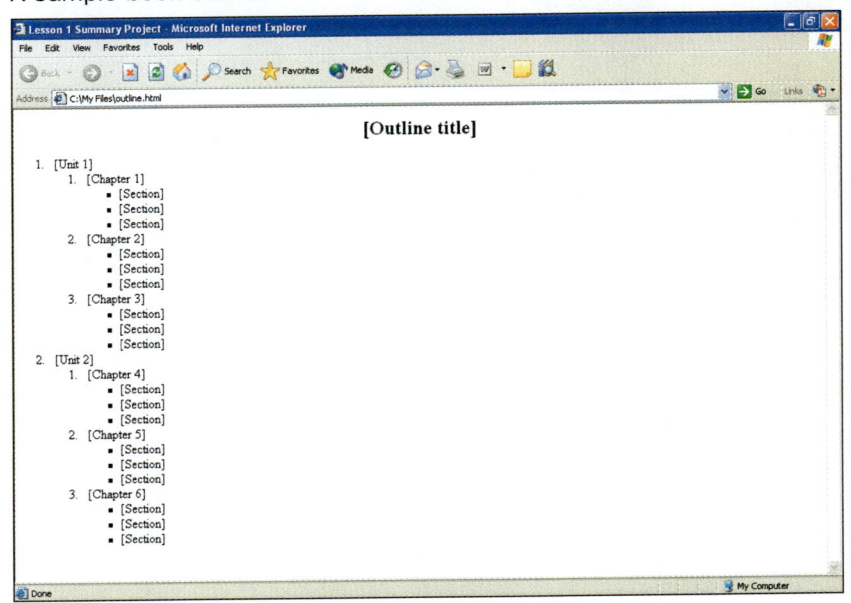

Project Requirements

- Your outline must have a title that is centered at the top of the page.
- Your outline must contain at least two units in an ordered list.
- Your outline must contain at least three chapters per unit, also ordered.
- You outline must contain at least three sections per chapter – not ordered.

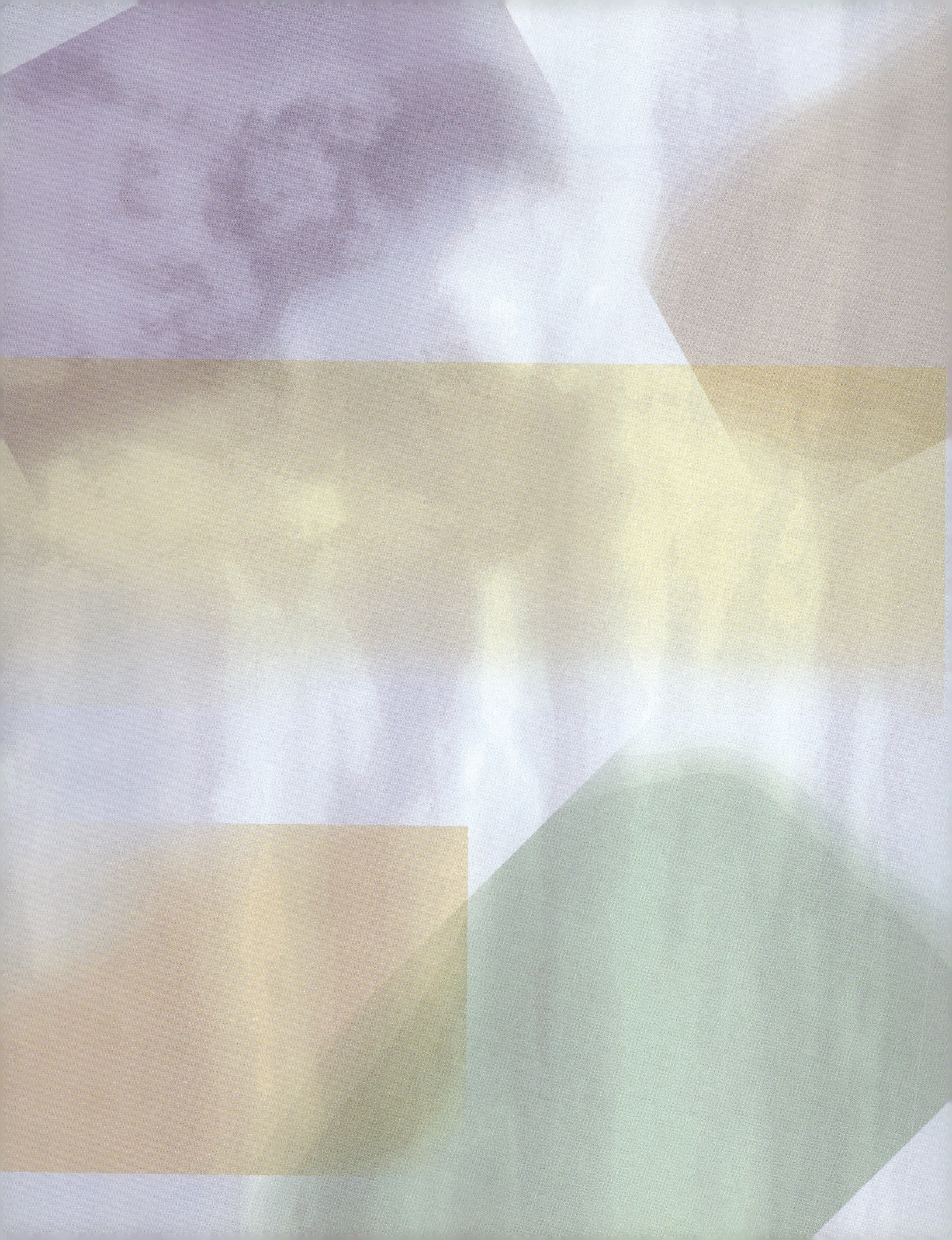

LESSON 2

HTML Organization Techniques

OBJECTIVES

Upon completion of this lesson, you should be able to:

- Organize page information with single and double spacing.
- Organize page information with lines.
- Implement attributes and values.
- Change Web page color defaults by altering attributes and values.
- Alter Web page text colors.
- Create a hyperlink to another spot within a Web page.
- Create a hyperlink to an URL or Web page anywhere on the WWW.
- Create a hyperlink to another Web page on your own computer.

Estimated Time: 1.5 hours

VOCABULARY

Attribute

Fonts

Hexadecimal

Hyperlinks

Hypertext links

Hypertext Transfer Protocol (HTTP)

Uniform Resource Locator (URL)

Value

Creating Better Web Pages

The World Wide Web is a creation of hundreds of thousands of people who are constantly creating, improving, and posting exciting Web pages. The Web is a place to be totally creative. All you need to join in the fun is a little knowledge of HTML and JavaScript. With these tools in your bag of tricks, you will be limited only by your imagination.

As you have surfed the Web, you have seen wonderfully exciting Web pages, and you have seen other pages that fall flat. The main difference between a great and a dull page comes down to the little things—the choice of lettering colors, pictures, and the selection of elements that help with the overall organization of the pages.

You can use many HTML techniques to make your pages perfectly presentable. These are single and double spacing techniques and other specialized organizing tags that can make any Web page easy to read. For example, Web pages can be made more appealing by adding space between paragraphs or by placing lines between different sections of the Web page. Changing the colors of your text and page background can also make an HTML document more appealing. Color choices are extremely important. There is nothing uglier in cyberspace than a Web page that mixes all the wrong colors. Use just the right colors, and your page will be fabulous.

Fonts, or the style of lettering, can be altered. Every font has a style all its own. Here are some samples of the most common fonts:

This is Times New Roman.

This is Arial.

This is Courier.

Hypertext links help make Web pages interesting and easy to navigate. *Hyperlinks*, as they are often called, allow users to click and zoom off to another place on the Web, to another page users have created, or to a spot within the current document. If you have a lot of information on a single page, creating an index can help your reader hyper-jump to the exact information for which they are looking.

As you learn the new HTML elements taught in this lesson, you will be introduced to new ideas on how to organize your Web pages.

Single and Double Spacing

Most early Web pages, before 1995, are best described as long, boring collections of words. Early versions of HTML supplied only the simplest ways to break text into readable sections.

That has changed. There is no longer any reason to create a boring, hard-to-read Web page. In the following Step-by-Step, you'll see firsthand how to improve the readability and organization of your page.

STEP-BY-STEP 2.1

1. Open Notepad, SimpleText, or your word processing software.

Lesson 2 HTML Organization Techniques

HTML BASICS **35**

STEP-BY-STEP 2.1 Continued

2. Key the HTML Web page information exactly as shown in Figure 2-1.

> **Note**
> If you are using Notepad, select the **Word Wrap** option from the **Format** menu before you enter the text.

FIGURE 2-1
Enter these tags and words exactly as shown

```
<HTML>
<TITLE>HTML and JavaScript</TITLE>

<BODY>
<CENTER><H1>Organizing Tags</H1></CENTER>

There are many ways to organize a Web page. This Web page will organize text, hypertext links, colors, and fonts. You'll also demonstrate single spacing, double spacing, and the use of line breaks.

This Web page will display how to organize Web pages in a number of ways using:

Powerful Lines
Hyperlinks to HTML and JavaScript Sources
Hyperlinks to Previously Created Web Pages
Fancy Fonts
Perfect Pictures
Orderly Tables
Extraordinary Extras

</BODY>
</HTML>
```

3. Save the file as you learned to save in Step-by-Step 1.3 with the name **six.html** or **six.htm**.

STEP-BY-STEP 2.1 Continued

4. Open your Web browser and view your page. It should look messy, as in Figure 2-2. (Refer back to Step-by-Step 1.3 if you need a reminder on how to view an HTML file in your Web browser.) Notice that while the page may have looked organized when you entered it in HTML, the organization of the page falls apart on the Web without a few organizing tags. The use of a few selected tags can really clean up a page. The two easiest tags you can use to organize a page are the <P></P>, or paragraph, tags, and the <BR>, or break tag. The <P></P> tags create a double space around the text. The <BR> tag creates a single-spaced break.

FIGURE 2-2
An unorganized Web page

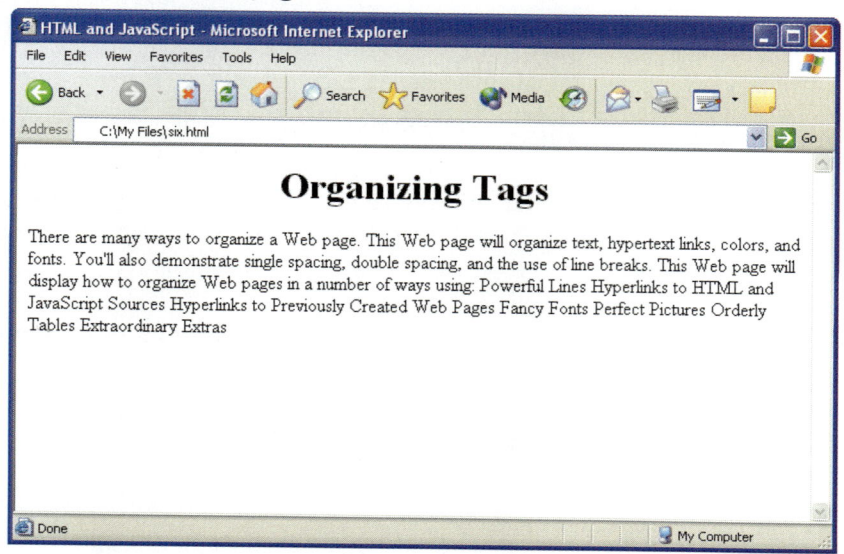

5. Open your **six.html** or **six.htm** file, if necessary, in your word processor, Notepad, or SimpleText.

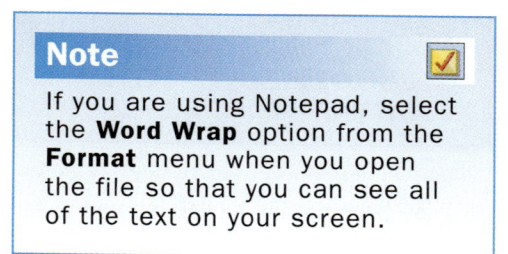

> **Note**
>
> If you are using Notepad, select the **Word Wrap** option from the **Format** menu when you open the file so that you can see all of the text on your screen.

Lesson 2 HTML Organization Techniques

HTML BASICS 37

STEP-BY-STEP 2.1 Continued

6. Add the <P></P> and <BR> tags, as marked in bold in Figure 2-3.

FIGURE 2-3
Enter the <P></P> and <BR> tags.

```
<HTML>
<TITLE>HTML and JavaScript</TITLE>

<BODY>
<CENTER><H1>Organizing Tags</H1></CENTER>

<P>There are many ways to organize a Web page. This Web page will organize text, hypertext links, colors, and fonts. You'll also demonstrate single spacing, double spacing, and the use of line breaks. </P>

<P>This Web page will display how to organize Web pages in a number of ways using: </P>

<BR>Powerful Lines
<BR>Hyperlinks to HTML and JavaScript Sources
<BR>Hyperlinks to Previously Created Web Pages
<BR>Fancy Fonts
<BR>Perfect Pictures
<BR>Orderly Tables
<BR>Extraordinary Extras

</BODY>
</HTML>
```

7. Use the **Save As** option to save your reorganized file as **seven.html** or **seven.htm**.

STEP-BY-STEP 2.1 Continued

8. Review your work. It should look much better this time, similar to Figure 2-4.

FIGURE 2-4
<P></P> and <BR> tags clean up a Web page

Organizing Tags

There are many ways to organize a Web page. This Web page will organize text, hypertext links, colors, and fonts. You'll also demonstrate single spacing, double spacing, and the use of line breaks.

This Web page will display how to organize Web pages in a number of ways using:

Powerful Lines
Hyperlinks to HTML and JavaScript Sources
Hyperlinks to Previously Created Web Pages
Fancy Fonts
Perfect Pictures
Orderly Tables
Extraordinary Extras

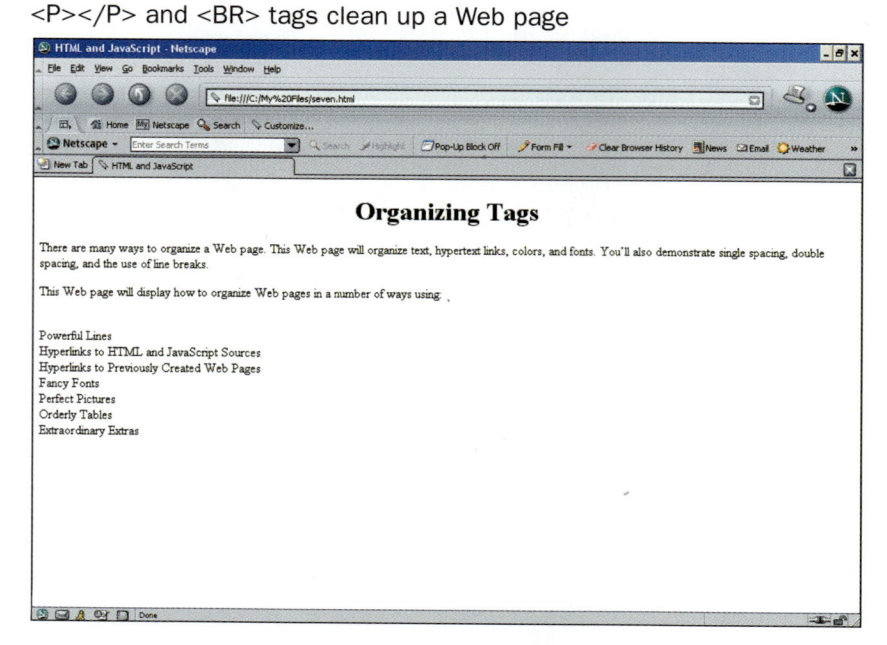

9. Continue to the next section, or close your software and shut down your computer if you're finished for the day.

Lines and Background Colors

HTML tags can be enhanced. Take the <BODY> tag, for instance. You can add commands to the body tag that will dramatically change the look of your Web page. For example, to change the background color of your Web page, you can add the background *attribute* (or special quality) and give the tag a color *value* (or a definition of the attribute), as shown in Figure 2-5.

Attributes and values are powerful tools to help you organize your Web pages. One of the most widely used tags is the <HR> or Horizontal Rule. This tag simply creates a horizontal line across the page. You can add attributes to change the size and shape of the horizontal rule as well.

FIGURE 2-5
Changing background colors

```
            Attribute    Value
<BODY BGCOLOR=YELLOW>
```

STEP-BY-STEP 2.2

1. Open your **seven.html** or **seven.htm** file for text editing, if necessary.

2. Enter **BGCOLOR=YELLOW** inside the BODY tag near the top of your Web page, as shown in bold in Figure 2-5.

3. Save your work as **eight.html** or **eight.htm**.

4. View these changes in your Web browser. Your page should turn yellow.

5. Experiment. Change the background color value to **BLUE, GREEN, RED, WHITE**, or another color of your choice.

STEP-BY-STEP 2.2 Continued

6. Switch back to your **eight.html** or **eight.htm** file. Enter the various <HR> tags, attributes, and values as marked in bold in Figure 2-6 near the bottom of the page before the </BODY> tag.

FIGURE 2-6
Adding background colors and lines

```
<HTML>
<TITLE>HTML and JavaScript</TITLE>

<BODY BGCOLOR=YELLOW>
<CENTER><H1>Organizing Tags</H1></CENTER>

<P>There are many ways to organize a Web page. This Web page will organize text, hypertext links, colors, and fonts. You'll also demonstrate single spacing, double spacing, and the use of line breaks. </P>

<P>This Web page will display how to organize Web pages in a number of ways using: </P>

<BR>Powerful Lines
<BR>Hyperlinks to HTML and JavaScript Sources
<BR>Hyperlinks to Previously Created Web Pages
<BR>Fancy Fonts
<BR>Perfect Pictures
<BR>Orderly Tables
<BR>Extraordinary Extras
<HR>

<P><H2>Powerful Lines</H2></P>

A Horizontal Rule tag 50% wide and 10 pixels high.
<HR WIDTH=50% SIZE=10>

A Horizontal Rule tag 25% wide and 20 pixels high.
<HR WIDTH=25% SIZE=20>

A Horizontal Rule tag 10% wide and 30 pixels high.
<HR WIDTH=10% SIZE=30>

A Horizontal Rule tag without attributes and values.
<HR>

</BODY>
</HTML>
```

7. Save your file as **nine.html** or **nine.htm**.

Lesson 2 HTML Organization Techniques

HTML BASICS 41

STEP-BY-STEP 2.2 Continued

8. View the horizontal lines in your Web browser. Your page should look like Figure 2-7.

FIGURE 2-7
Powerful lines

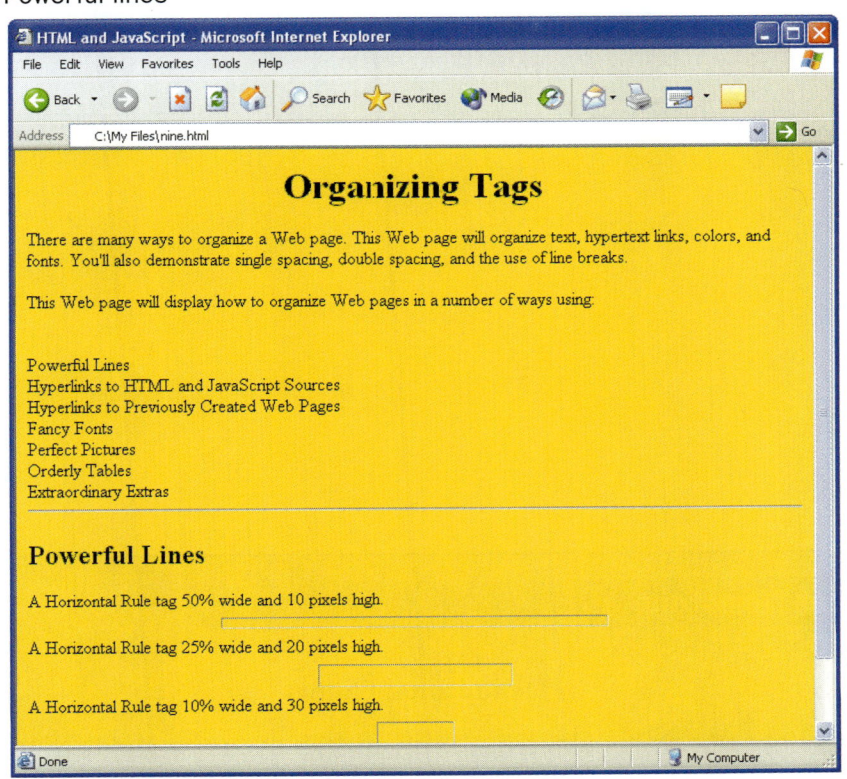

9. Continue to the next section, or close your software and shut down your computer if you're finished for the day.

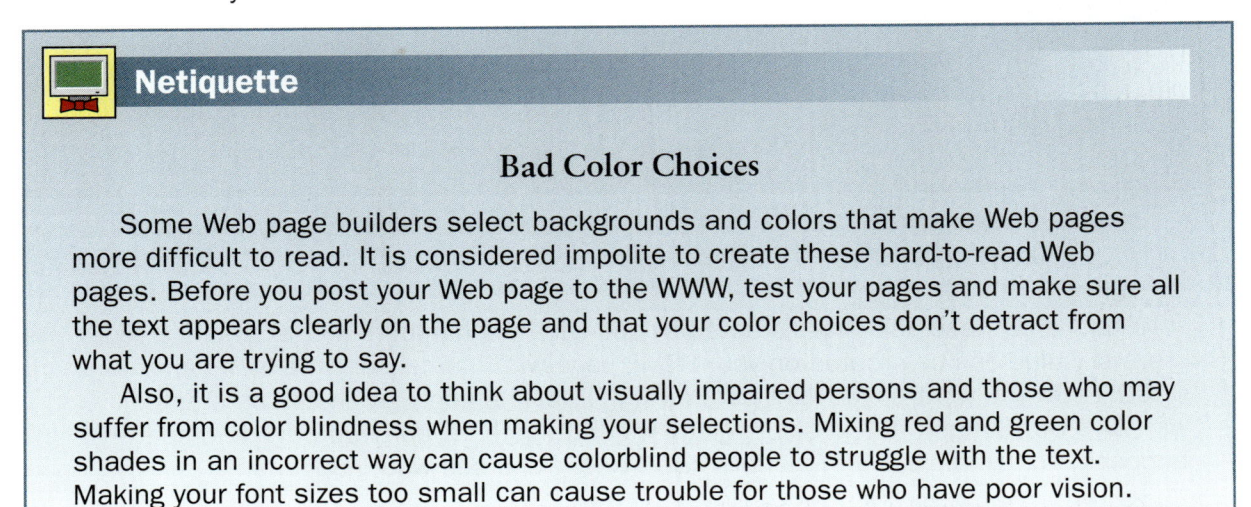

Netiquette

Bad Color Choices

Some Web page builders select backgrounds and colors that make Web pages more difficult to read. It is considered impolite to create these hard-to-read Web pages. Before you post your Web page to the WWW, test your pages and make sure all the text appears clearly on the page and that your color choices don't detract from what you are trying to say.

Also, it is a good idea to think about visually impaired persons and those who may suffer from color blindness when making your selections. Mixing red and green color shades in an incorrect way can cause colorblind people to struggle with the text. Making your font sizes too small can cause trouble for those who have poor vision. Using a dark background with dark letters can make a page difficult for anyone to read.

Hyperlinks Inside Your Document

Web pages became popular because they could link easily to other pages or to various sections inside a document at the speed of an electron. Hyperlinks are easy to use but a little difficult to understand at first.

To use a hyperlink, just click on the link. Links may be pictures or words that are underlined and appear in a different color, as shown in Figure 2-8.

Internet Milestone

Hexadecimal Colors

Computers speak only in numbers. Values are expressed as numbers that the computer understands. Color values can be carefully controlled and changed to match virtually every color in the rainbow by using special numerical or **hexadecimal** values for certain colors. The invention of hexadecimal is one of the greatest advances in computing. Hexadecimal digits operate on a base-16 number system rather than the base-10 number system we humans normally use. Hexadecimal numbers use the letters A, B, C, D, E, and F along with the numbers 0 to 9 to create 16 different digits. For example, look at the following color values expressed as numbers:

White =#FFFFFF
Green =#00FF00
Black =#000000
Blue =#0000FF
Red =#FF0000
Yellow =#FFFF00

Shades of these colors are created by changing the numbers. For example, a really great sky blue can be created on your HTML page with the hexadecimal number 00CCFF. Do you want a nice light purple? Try FF95FF. An ugly green can be created with AAFF00. Substitute text color values with numbers in your Web page and see what happens. For example, try this in the <BODY> tag and see what happens:

BGCOLOR=#AAFF00 VLINK=#FF95FF TEXT=#00CCFF LINK=#FFFF00

FIGURE 2-8
A hyperlink text

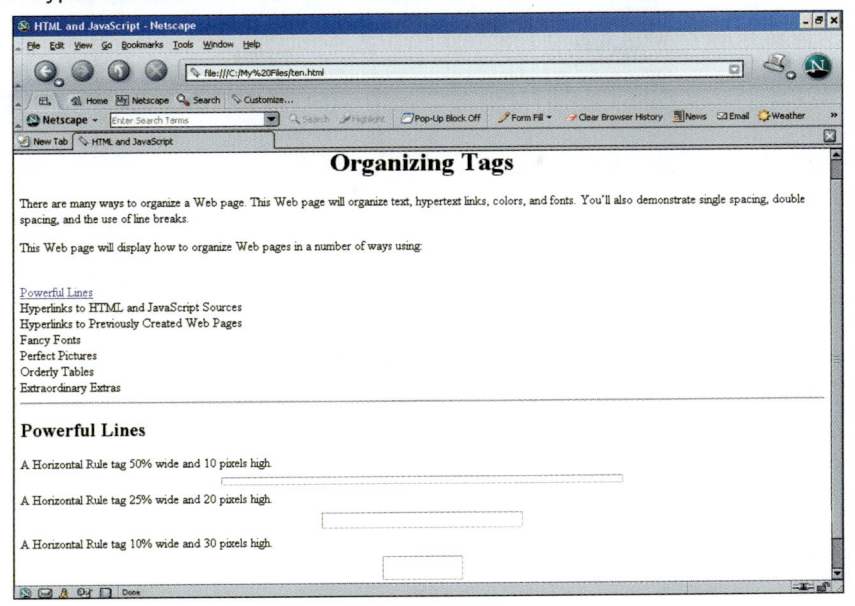

Hyperlinks are created with special tags called anchor tags. The tag has several parts. The opening and closing tags are called the anchor or link tags and look like this:

<A HREF="insert location of file"></A>

Link or anchor tags are fairly useless unless you define the place to which you are linking. There are several ways to use anchor tags. You can:

- Link to another spot within your own document.
- Link to an URL or Web page anywhere on the WWW.
- Link to another Web page on your own computer.

In Step-by-Step 2.4, you will link to the WWW, and in Step-by-Step 2.5, you will create hyperlinks to all the Web pages you have created so far. In this activity, we will start linking within your HTML page.

These internal hyperlinks help users navigate between important parts of your Web page. The first <A> tag you insert will create a hypertext link to a location within your document. You will create the tag in Step 3. The attribute is HREF= and the value is "#POWERFUL". The quotation marks are necessary, as is the #, or pound sign.

The second anchor tag will identify the exact location in your Web page to which you want to link. In Step 4, you will create a tag with the attribute NAME= and a value called "POWERFUL" with quotation marks.

STEP-BY-STEP 2.3

1. Open your **nine.html** or **nine.htm** file for text editing, if necessary.

2. Change the background color back to white by changing the **BGCOLOR** attribute from **YELLOW** to **WHITE**.

3. Add the following anchor **<A></A>** tags before and after the first Powerful Lines list item, as shown in Figure 2-9.

<A HREF="#POWERFUL">Powerful Lines</A>

4. Insert the following anchor **<A></A>** tags around the second Powerful Lines list item, as shown here and marked in bold in Figure 2-9.

    <P><H2><A NAME="POWERFUL">Powerful Lines</A></H2></P>

5. Save your new file as **ten.html** or **ten.htm**.

> **Note**
>
> The pound sign # can be created by holding the Shift key down and pressing the number 3. The quotation marks (") are created by holding down Shift and pressing the single quote (') key.

Net Ethics

Respect the WWW

What you write in a Web page shouldn't be offensive to others. You're responsible for what you create and post on the WWW. RESPECT the Web. When creating your Web pages, consider these guidelines:

R = Responsibility: Assume personal responsibility and create only ethical and appropriate pages.

E = Everybody: Try to create Web pages that everybody can enjoy, appreciate, and consider of value.

S = Simplicity: Make your Web pages easy to navigate. Make information simple to find.

P = Purpose: Have a clear purpose for every Web page you put on the Web. Don't post unnecessary pages.

E = Ethical: Make sure all the content of every Web page you post corresponds to your values and has a beneficial purpose.

C = Correct: Make sure all the words on your page are spelled correctly, all the sentences are written correctly, and all the hyperlinks work.

T = Totally worth visiting: Try to create pages that others will think are totally worth their time to visit.

Lesson 2 HTML Organization Techniques   HTML BASICS   45

STEP-BY-STEP 2.3 Continued

6. View the changes in your Web browser. Your link should look like the sample in Figure 2-8. When you click this link, you should jump down the page to the Powerful Lines heading in your document.

7. Continue to the next section, or close your software and shut down your computer if you're finished for the day.

FIGURE 2-9
Insert background color and internal linking tags

```
<HTML>
<TITLE>HTML and JavaScript</TITLE>

<BODY BGCOLOR=WHITE>
<CENTER><H1>Organizing Tags</H1></CENTER>

<P>There are many ways to organize a Web page. This Web page will organize text, hypertext links, colors, and fonts. You'll also demonstrate single spacing, double spacing, and the use of line breaks. </P>

<P>This Web page will display how to organize Web pages in a number of ways using: </P>

<BR><A HREF="#POWERFUL">Powerful Lines</A>
<BR>Hyperlinks to HTML and JavaScript Sources
<BR>Hyperlinks to Previously Created Web Pages
<BR>Fancy Fonts
<BR>Perfect Pictures
<BR>Orderly Tables
<BR>Extraordinary Extras
<HR>

<P><H2><A NAME="POWERFUL">Powerful Lines</A></H2></P>

A Horizontal Rule tag 50% wide and 10 pixels high.
<HR WIDTH=50% SIZE=10>

A Horizontal Rule tag 25% wide and 20 pixels high.
<HR WIDTH=25% SIZE=20>

A Horizontal Rule tag 10% wide and 30 pixels high.
<HR WIDTH=10% SIZE=30>

A Horizontal Rule tag without attributes and values.
<HR>

</BODY>
</HTML>
```

Creating Hypertext Links to the Web

The thing that first made the WWW popular was the ability to jump from one page to another anywhere in the world. Before you can do this, however, you must know all about URLs. **URL** stands for **Uniform Resource Locator**. URLs allow a Web browser to pinpoint an exact file on the Web. The concept is really quite simple. Have you ever seen an URL similar to this sample?

http://www.course.com/webpagefolder/anotherfolder/afile.html

When you enter an URL into your HTML Web page, you're identifying a path to a specific HTML file located somewhere online. This file may be on your local computer or somewhere on the Web.

You often can see the name of the file at the end of an URL. Look at the end of our sample URL. The filename *afile.html* is the name of an HTML file (afile). The .html extension identifies the file as an HTML document that your Web browser can display.

However, before you can get to *afile.html*, you need to know the path or the way to this filename. The key to finding the filename's path is by looking at its URL or Web address. Let's see what this means by breaking down the sample URL into its various parts.

In some URLs, you may see the letters *http* followed by a colon and a couple of slashes. The *http://* tells your network how to transfer or move the files you are requesting. **HTTP** stands for **Hypertext Transfer Protocol**. A protocol is a communication system that is used to transfer data over networks. It is like a secret digital language that Web servers use to communicate with Web browsers.

The second part of the address, *www.course.com*, is the actual name of the server (or Web computer) that hosts the Web page for which you are looking. The *www* stands for World Wide Web. The www tells you that the server uses Web technology. The *.course* part is the name of the company that maintains the Web server. In this case, course is short for Course Technology. The *.com* says that this is a commercial or business site. You may see other addresses that are marked as *.edu* for education, *.gov* for government Web sites, or *.biz* for business sites.

Lesson 2 HTML Organization Techniques

HTML BASICS 47

The slashes and names in the rest of the URL (/webpagefolder/anotherfolder/) represent folders on the Web server. These are also called subdirectories. You have subdirectories on your computer also. Figure 2-10 shows how folders are organized on a Windows computer. All computers use some sort of folder system to organize files. If you want to find a file on a computer, you need to know the path through the many possible folders in which the file is stored. Knowing the path is the key to finding the Web page you want.

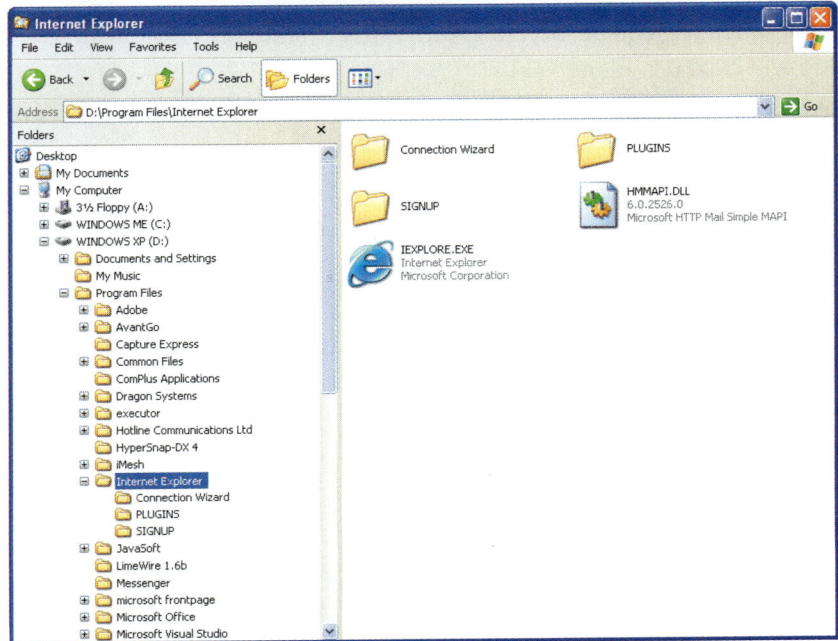

FIGURE 2-10
A Windows folder or directory organization

Before you can find a Web site's welcome page, you need to know the URL. In this Step-by-Step, you'll enter URLs for some of the most important companies in the race to create a better, more exciting Web. Many of the sites have information on HTML, JavaScript, and other important Web tools. They include:

http://www.microsoft.com

http://www.sun.com

http://home.netscape.com

http://www.oracle.com

STEP-BY-STEP 2.4

1. Open your **ten.html** or **ten.htm** file for text editing, if necessary.

2. Create a hypertext link (as shown here and in bold in Figure 2-11) from the list near the top of the page to the new section you are creating.

`<BR><A HREF="#HYPERLINKS">Hyperlinks to HTML and JavaScript Sources</A>`

STEP-BY-STEP 2.4 Continued

3. Add a new level 2 heading with the words **Hyperlinks to HTML and JavaScript Sources** just below the last <HR> tag of your Web page and just before the </BODY> tag as shown here and in Figure 2-11. Include the <A NAME> tag so that you can create an internal hypertext link from the link you created in Step 2.

<P><H2><A NAME="HYPERLINKS">Hyperlinks to HTML and JavaScript Sources</A></H2></P>

4. Below your new heading and before the </BODY> tag, create the following hypertext links exactly as shown here and in bold in Figure 2-11.

```
<BR><A HREF="http://www.microsoft.com">Microsoft</A>
<BR><A HREF="http://home.netscape.com">Netscape</A>
<BR><A HREF="http://www.sun.com">Sun</A>
<BR><A HREF="http://www.oracle.com">Oracle</A>
<HR>
```

Lesson 2 HTML Organization Techniques   **HTML BASICS** 49

STEP-BY-STEP 2.4 Continued

FIGURE 2-11
Hypertext linking tags

```
<HTML>
<TITLE>HTML and JavaScript</TITLE>

<BODY BGCOLOR=WHITE>
<CENTER><H1>Organizing Tags</H1></CENTER>

<P>There are many ways to organize a Web page. This Web page will organize text,
hypertext links, colors, and fonts. You'll also demonstrate single spacing, double spac-
ing, and the use of line breaks. </P>

<P>This Web page will display how to organize Web pages in a number of ways using: </P>

<BR><A HREF="#POWERFUL">Powerful Lines</A>
<BR><A HREF="#HYPERLINKS">Hyperlinks to HTML and JavaScript Sources</A>
<BR>Hyperlinks to Previously Created Web Pages
<BR>Fancy Fonts
<BR>Perfect Pictures
<BR>Orderly Tables
<BR>Extraordinary Extras
<HR>

<P><H2><A NAME="POWERFUL">Powerful Lines</A></H2></P>

A Horizontal Rule tag 50% wide and 10 pixels high.
<HR WIDTH=50% SIZE=10>

A Horizontal Rule tag 25% wide and 20 pixels high.
<HR WIDTH=25% SIZE=20>

A Horizontal Rule tag 10% wide and 30 pixels high.
<HR WIDTH=10% SIZE=30>

A Horizontal Rule tag without attributes and values.
<HR>

<P><H2><A NAME="HYPERLINKS">Hyperlinks to HTML and JavaScript Sources
</A></H2></P>

<BR><A HREF="http://www.microsoft.com">Microsoft</A>
<BR><A HREF="http://home.netscape.com">Netscape</A>
<BR><A HREF="http://www.sun.com">Sun</A>
<BR><A HREF="http://www.oracle.com">Oracle</A>
<HR>

</BODY>
</HTML>
```

STEP-BY-STEP 2.4 Continued

5. Your entire page of tags should appear like those in Figure 2-11. Save your work as **eleven.html** or **eleven.htm**.

6. View your work in your Web browser. Your new links should look like Figure 2-12.

FIGURE 2-12
Hyperlinks in your Web browser

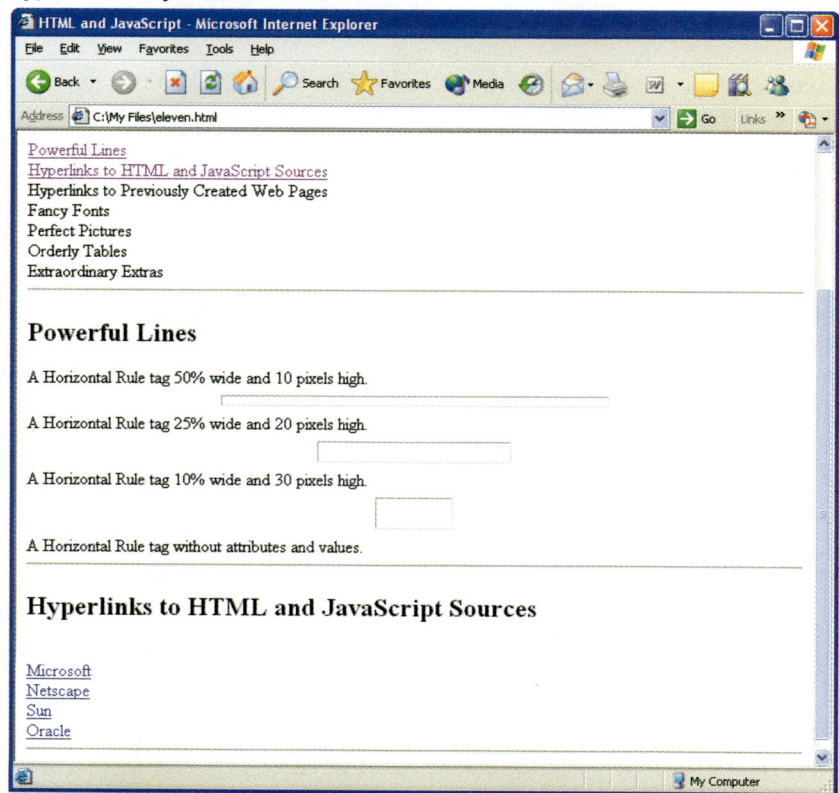

7. If you have a live connection to the Web, try your links and see if they work! If your links don't work properly, carefully review your tags and make any necessary corrections. Save your work again. Then reload or refresh your page in your Web browser and try again.

8. Continue to the next section or close your software and shut down your computer if you're finished for the day.

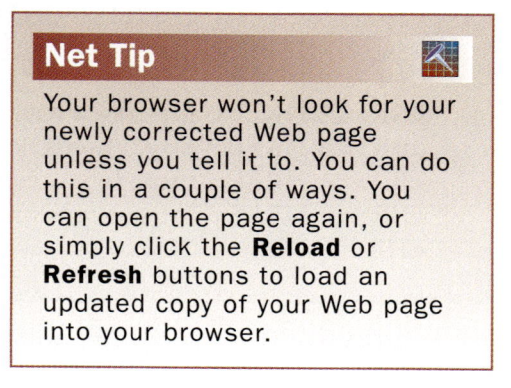

Net Tip

Your browser won't look for your newly corrected Web page unless you tell it to. You can do this in a couple of ways. You can open the page again, or simply click the **Reload** or **Refresh** buttons to load an updated copy of your Web page into your browser.

Lesson 2 HTML Organization Techniques

Linking to Pages You Have Already Created

In this Step-by-Step, you'll link to the first 11 HTML pages you have created in this book. Keeping track of all your pages in this way will help you quickly review the progress you have made.

STEP-BY-STEP 2.5

1. Open your **eleven.html** or **eleven.htm** file, if necessary.

2. Create a hypertext link from your list near the top of the page to the new section you are creating. The text to be entered is shown below and in bold in Figure 2-13.

`<BR><A HREF="#PREVIOUS">Hyperlinks to Previously Created Web Pages</A>`

3. As shown in Figure 2-13, add a new level 2 heading called **Hyperlinks to Previously Created Web Pages** just below the HR tag you added in the previous exercise, and just before the </BODY> tag. Include the <A NAME> tag so you can link to this exact spot from the tag you created in Step 3.

`<P><H2><A NAME="PREVIOUS">Hyperlinks to Previously Created Web Pages </A></H2></P>`

4. Below the new heading near the end of your document, create the hypertext links exactly as shown here and in bold in Figure 2-13.

```
<BR><A HREF="one.html">one</A>
<BR><A HREF="two.html">two</A>
<BR><A HREF="three.html">three</A>
<BR><A HREF="four.html">four</A>
<BR><A HREF="five.html">five</A>
<BR><A HREF="six.html">six</A>
<BR><A HREF="seven.html">seven</A>
<BR><A HREF="eight.html">eight</A>
<BR><A HREF="nine.html">nine</A>
<BR><A HREF="ten.html">ten</A>
<BR><A HREF="eleven.html">eleven</A>
<HR>
```

HTML BASICS

STEP-BY-STEP 2.5 Continued

5. Your entire page of tags should now appear like those in Figure 2-13. Save your work as **twelve.html** or **twelve.htm**.

FIGURE 2-13
Creating links to Web pages you have created

```
<HTML>
<TITLE>HTML and JavaScript</TITLE>

<BODY BGCOLOR=WHITE>
<CENTER><H1>Organizing Tags</H1></CENTER>

<P>There are many ways to organize a Web page. This Web page will organize text, hypertext links, colors, and fonts. You'll also demonstrate single spacing, double spacing, and the use of line breaks. </P>

<P>This Web page will display how to organize Web pages in a number of ways using: </P>

<BR><A HREF="#POWERFUL">Powerful Lines</A>
<BR><A HREF="#HYPERLINKS">Hyperlinks to HTML and JavaScript Sources</A>
<BR><A HREF="#PREVIOUS">Hyperlinks to Previously Created Web Pages</A>
<BR>Fancy Fonts
<BR>Perfect Pictures
<BR>Orderly Tables
<BR>Extraordinary Extras
<HR>

<P><H2><A NAME="POWERFUL">Powerful Lines</A></H2></P>

A Horizontal Rule tag 50% wide and 10 pixels high.
<HR WIDTH=50% SIZE=10>

A Horizontal Rule tag 25% wide and 20 pixels high.
<HR WIDTH=25% SIZE=20>

A Horizontal Rule tag 10% wide and 30 pixels high.
<HR WIDTH=10% SIZE=30>

A Horizontal Rule tag without attributes and values.
<HR>

<P><H2><A NAME="HYPERLINKS">Hyperlinks to HTML and JavaScript Sources</A></H2></P>

<BR><A HREF="http://www.microsoft.com">Microsoft</A>
<BR><A HREF="http://home.netscape.com">Netscape</A>
<BR><A HREF="http://www.sun.com">Sun</A>
<BR><A HREF="http://www.oracle.com">Oracle</A>
```

Lesson 2 HTML Organization Techniques

STEP-BY-STEP 2.5 Continued

FIGURE 2-13 (Continued)
Creating links to Web pages you have created

```
<HR>

<P><H2><A NAME="PREVIOUS">Hyperlinks to Previously Created Web Pages </A></H2></P>

<BR><A HREF="one.html">one</A>
<BR><A HREF="two.html"">two</A>
<BR><A HREF="three.html">three</A>
<BR><A HREF="four.html">four</A>
<BR><A HREF="five.html">five</A>
<BR><A HREF="six.html">six</A>
<BR><A HREF="seven.html">seven</A>
<BR><A HREF="eight.html">eight</A>
<BR><A HREF="nine.html">nine</A>
<BR><A HREF="ten.html">ten</A>
<BR><A HREF="eleven.html">eleven</A>
<HR>

</BODY>
</HTML>
```

STEP-BY-STEP 2.5 Continued

6. View your work in your Web browser. Your new links should look like Figure 2-14. Test each link and make sure they all work. Make any corrections that are necessary.

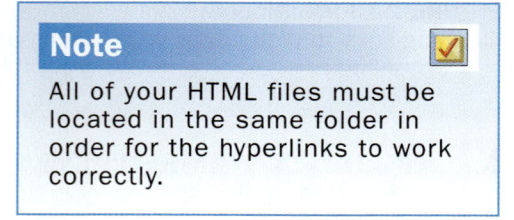

> **Note**
>
> All of your HTML files must be located in the same folder in order for the hyperlinks to work correctly.

FIGURE 2-14
Links to previously created Web pages

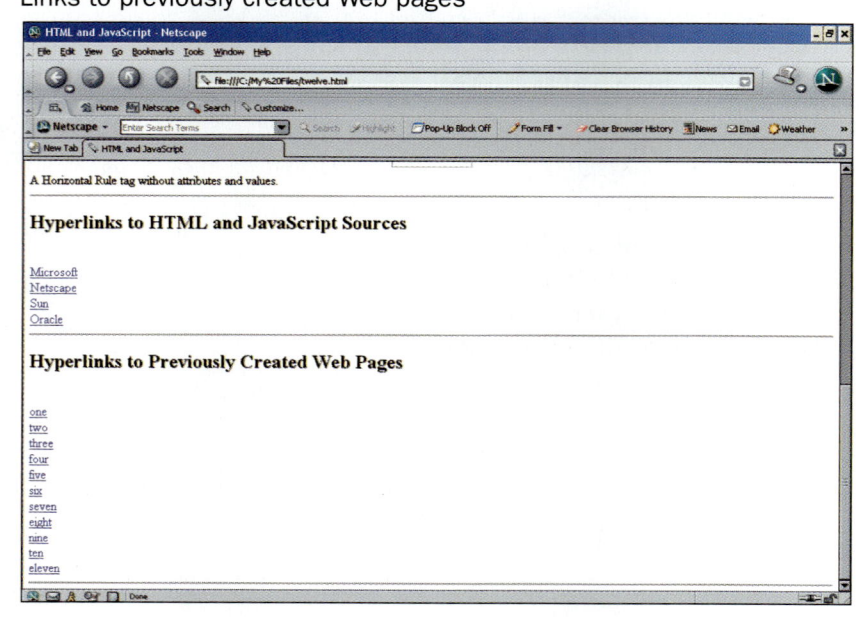

7. Continue to the next section or close your software and shut down your computer if you're finished for the day.

Coloring Text

While surfing the Web, have you noticed that the text colors often change from page to page? In Step-by-Step 2.1, you changed the background color of your Web page by inserting the YELLOW value into the BGCOLOR= attribute in the <BODY> tag. Then you changed the background to several other colors. Changing text color is just as easy.

Table 2-1 shows the three basic types of text color you can change.

TABLE 2-1
Text color

TYPE OF TEXT	ATTRIBUTE
1. The text itself	TEXT=
2. The hypertext link color	LINK=
3. The visited link color (or the links you have already selected)	VLINK=

Lesson 2 HTML Organization Techniques

HTML BASICS

STEP-BY-STEP 2.6

1. Open your **twelve.html** or **twelve.htm** file, if necessary.

2. In the body tag at the beginning of the Web page, leave the BGCOLOR as WHITE, but insert **TEXT=BLUE, LINK=RED**, and **VLINK=GREEN**, as shown in Figure 2-15.

FIGURE 2-15
Changing the text color on a Web page

```
<HTML>
<TITLE> HTML and JavaScript </TITLE>

<BODY BGCOLOR=WHITE TEXT=BLUE LINK=RED VLINK=GREEN>
```

3. Save your work as **thirteen.html** or **thirteen.htm**. View your work in your Web browser. Your page should appear with blue text, red hyperlinks, and green visited links on a white background as seen in Figure 2-16.

4. Continue to the Summary section or close your software and shut down your computer if you're finished for the day.

FIGURE 2-16
Changing text colors

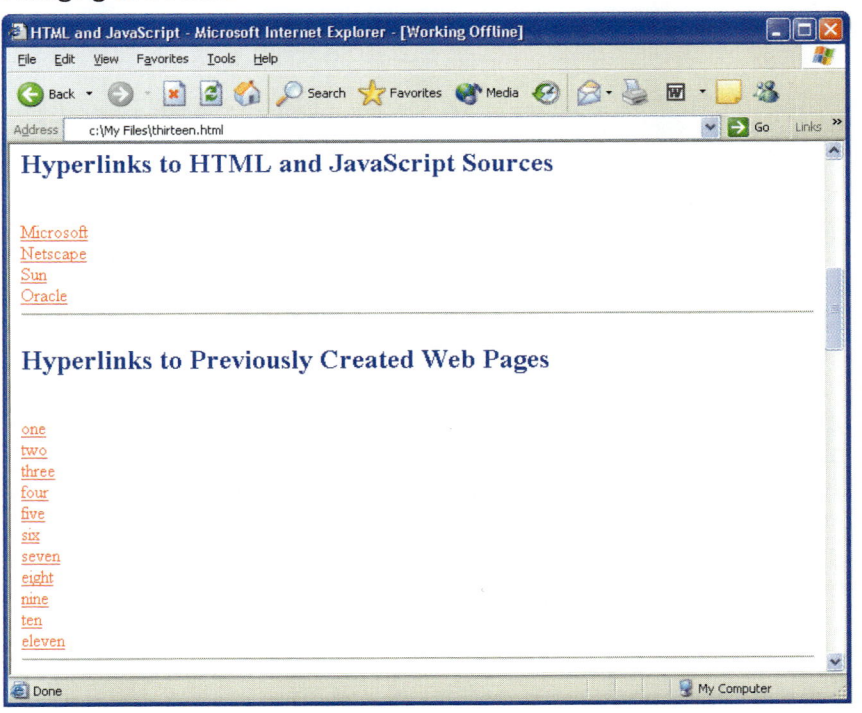

Perfect Proofreading Tips

Proofreading HTML tags can be difficult. Even the slightest error can drastically change the look of a Web page. Here are some common errors to look for:

- Make sure all your angle brackets < > are facing in the proper direction.

- Often, Web page writers misuse the shift key when making angle brackets or creating a slash. This results in a comma, a period, or a question mark where the slash or angle brackets should appear.

- If all the text appears centered, perhaps you forgot to use the close </CENTER> tag.

- If you want a double space instead of a single space, use a <P></P> tag instead of a <BR> tag.

- If bullets appear long after a list, perhaps you forgot the close unordered list tag </UL>.

Net Fun

Another fun tag is the marquee tag. Anything you put between the marquee tags, <MARQUEE></MARQUEE>, will scroll across the screen like a stock market ticker. The tag was designed for the Internet Explorer browser by Microsoft, and doesn't work on every browser. Experiment, and see what happens!

Internet Milestone

HTML Standards

HTML is a powerful tool because it allows all kinds of computers to display Web pages. With HTML, it doesn't matter if you're running a Macintosh or a Windows machine. You can even be on a Linux or UNIX workstation or some other type of computer. The reason HTML Web pages can be viewed by all types of computers is because there are standards that all Web browsers understand. New standards and new HTML tags and commands are being added all the time. Each new tag is submitted to a standards committee for review. Every now and then enough new commands are added to HTML for a new version of HTML to be developed. These versions are marked by numbers: HTML 1, HTML 2, HTML 3, HTML 4, and so on. You can learn more about HTML standards and receive help expanding your HTML skills online. Go to your search portal and try these search words:

HTML
HTML Standards
HTML Standards Committee
HTML Learning
HTML Guides

Lesson 2 HTML Organization Techniques   HTML BASICS   57

SUMMARY

In this lesson, you learned:

- You can organize page information with single and double spacing.
- You can organize page information with lines.
- You can use attributes and values to improve Web page design.
- You can change color defaults, attributes, and values.
- You can create hypertext links to a spot in a Web document.
- You can create hypertext links to another page on the World Wide Web.
- You can create hypertext links to Web pages on your own computer.

VOCABULARY *Review*

Define the following terms:

Attribute	Hypertext links	Uniform Resource Locator
Fonts	Hypertext Transfer Protocol	(URL)
Hexadecimal	(HTTP)	Value
Hyperlinks		

REVIEW *Questions*

TRUE/FALSE

Circle T if the statement is true or F if the statement is false.

T   F   1. Hexadecimal numbers operate on a base-10 number system.

T   F   2. The <BR> tag creates a double-space around the text.

T   F   3. HREF is an attribute to the <A></A> anchor tag.

T   F   4. You can change the color of just about any text on your Web page.

T   F   5. The <HR> tag creates a single-space break.

FILL IN THE BLANK

Complete the following sentences by writing the correct word or words in the blanks provided.

1. The _____ tag creates text that scrolls across the screen.
2. You can _____ space in an HTML document with the <P> tag.

HTML BASICS

3. A(n) _____ is a communications system that is used to transfer data over networks.
4. A(n) _____ number lets you define a color with numbers and letters.
5. The _____ attribute changes a Web page's background color.

WRITTEN QUESTIONS

Write a brief answer to the following questions.

1. What tag allows text to scroll across the screen repeatedly?

2. What hexadecimal value will create the color yellow?

3. Which tag(s) do you know of that do not require a closing tag in order to work effectively?

4. What are three common HTML errors?

5. Why are there different versions of HTML?

PROJECTS

PROJECT 2-1

In the Teamwork activity from Lesson 1, you identified the greatest Web pages you could find. In this Project, GreatApplications, Inc., wants you to identify the five worst pages you can find. These are to be used in a training seminar to help new employees learn how to create high-quality Web pages. Your managers suggested that you surf the Web and find five examples of hard-to-read, unorganized, or boring Web pages to show new interns exactly what not to do.

Surf the Web looking for awful Web page examples. Record the title and URL of each page and list a few reasons why these pages are horrible!

TABLE 2-2
Examples of unorganized Web pages

TITLE THAT APPEARS IN THE TITLE BAR	WEB ADDRESS OR URL	REASONS WHY THIS PAGE IS BAD
1.		
2.		
3.		
4.		
5.		

TEAMWORK PROJECT

GreatApplications, Inc., is holding a design contest to see who can build the most informative and organized Web pages. Specifically, they are looking for a team that can create Web pages to introduce new products to customers over the Web.

The contest gives teams of three to five people two hours to create an informative Web page about a product of their choice. Form your team and brainstorm a new product to introduce. It could be a new DVD or a new computer game. It could be a new fashion or a new car. For the purpose of this contest, it doesn't really matter what product you pick, so don't take up too much of your time deciding what product you will use.

Create your team's Web page contest entry. Divide the writing responsibilities. Have one person enter the basic tags and serve as Webmaster. Each team member must research and write a portion of the Web page. Collaborate by editing and revising each other's writing and HTML tags. Use the techniques you have learned in this lesson to organize the information you wish to present.

WEB PROJECT

We all know that teamwork is important. However, are there times when teamwork is harder than working alone? Answer the following questions about teams creating Web pages together.

1. As you worked together on the Teamwork Project, what problems did you encounter?
2. How did you organize your team? How did you divide the work? Which team members were responsible for which activities?
3. Did teamwork create a better Web page? If so, how?
4. What advice would you give to other teams that are trying to create Web pages?

CRITICAL *Thinking*

Prepare a 100- to 250-word answer to each of the following questions.

ACTIVITY 2-1

Can you figure out how to create an internal hyperlink that will allow you to move from the bottom of your document to the very top? Use the steps you learned in Step-by-Step 2.3 to create a link just before the </BODY> tag that will link you to the top of the page. Your link should look like this: Top of Page. Why do you think a link back to the top of a page would be valuable?

ACTIVITY 2-2

What are your top 10 most important Web sites? What makes them important to you? Create a new HTML page that indexes and lists your most important personal Web pages. Call the page **My Web Resources**. Keep adding to your Web resources page as you work through this text.

SUMMARY *Project*

No matter what career you may choose for yourself later in life, it is very important to develop good communication skills. For example, everyone can benefit from learning how to write a well-formatted business letter. Use the HTML text formatting skills you learned in this lesson to develop a business letter to your teacher. When you are finished, your letter should have the general appearance of the sample letter shown in Figure 2-17.

Lesson 2 HTML Organization Techniques

FIGURE 2-17
A sample business letter

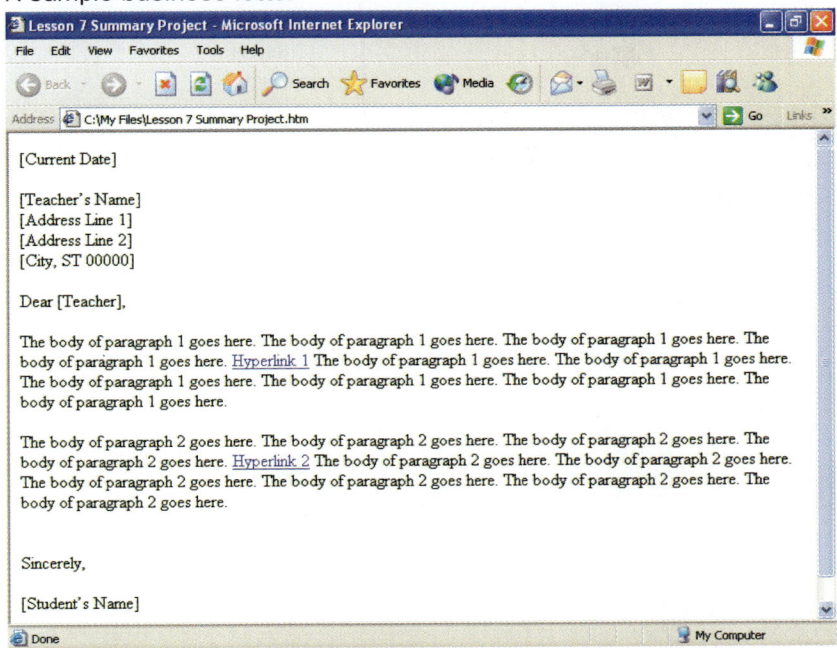

[Current Date]

[Teacher's Name]
[Address Line 1]
[Address Line 2]
[City, ST 00000]

Dear [Teacher],

The body of paragraph 1 goes here. The body of paragraph 1 goes here. The body of paragraph 1 goes here. The body of paragraph 1 goes here. Hyperlink 1 The body of paragraph 1 goes here. The body of paragraph 1 goes here. The body of paragraph 1 goes here. The body of paragraph 1 goes here. The body of paragraph 1 goes here. The body of paragraph 1 goes here.

The body of paragraph 2 goes here. The body of paragraph 2 goes here. The body of paragraph 2 goes here. The body of paragraph 2 goes here. Hyperlink 2 The body of paragraph 2 goes here. The body of paragraph 2 goes here. The body of paragraph 2 goes here. The body of paragraph 2 goes here. The body of paragraph 2 goes here. The body of paragraph 2 goes here.

Sincerely,

[Student's Name]

Project Requirements

- Your letter should have a date at the top of the page.
- The date should be followed by an address and a salutation.
- The main body of your letter must contain at least two full paragraphs.
- Your letter should end with a closing phrase and your own name.
- You must include at least one hyperlink per paragraph in your letter.
- The text should display in blue, and the hyperlinks should be red.
- Make sure that your letter maintains its formatting when you resize your browser window. (The spacing between paragraphs should remain consistent.)

LESSON 3

HTML Power Techniques

OBJECTIVES

Upon completion of this lesson, you should be able to:

- Control the size, style, and color of fonts.
- Download pictures from the Web.
- Insert pictures into your Web page.
- Change the size of graphics.
- Use tables to organize information.
- Turn pictures into hyperlinks.
- Insert a variety of data input options into a Web page.

Estimated Time: 1.5 hours

VOCABULARY

.gif

.jpg or .jpeg

Graphics Interchange Format

Joint Photographic Experts Group

Table cells

The Exciting Web

The Web is full of pictures, sounds, and movies that add interest to Web pages. Generally, there are two kinds of pictures, called graphics or images, on the World Wide Web. They include .gif files (Graphics Interchange Format) and .jpg or .jpeg (Joint Photographic Experts Group) files. The extensions .gif and .jpg help tell your browser that these files are pictures, not .html text files, and require special handling. We will discuss and define these files in more detail later in the lesson.

The more you learn about HTML, the more you can add exciting new effects and styles to your Web pages. As we mentioned in Lesson 2, fonts, or the style of letters, can be changed. Every font has a style all its own.

By using the <FONT> tag's many attributes and values, you can manipulate fonts in unlimited ways, as you will soon experience in this lesson.

Tables allow the parts of a Web page to be divided up, creating special spaces for each new element or piece of information you may want to include.

Tables, fonts, and pictures can add power to your pages. In this lesson, you will learn to manipulate the special HTML features. You'll also learn about some extraordinary input tags that will allow visitors to your Web page to interact with your Web page.

Font Attributes and Values

When you change text colors in the <BODY> tag, as you did in Step-by-Step 2.6 in Lesson 2, you change the color of your words for the entire page. If you want to have more control (that is, if you want to change the size, color, or style of a single paragraph, a single sentence, or even a single word) use the <FONT> tag.

Use <FONT> tag attributes to control:

- The size of words with the SIZE attribute <FONT SIZE=#>
- The style of words with the FACE attribute <FONT FACE=#>
- The color of words with the COLOR attribute <FONT COLOR=#>

STEP-BY-STEP 3.1

1. Open your **thirteen.html** or **thirteen.htm** file (from Lesson 2) for text editing.

2. Create a hypertext link in the list near the top of the page that will hyperlink to the new section you'll be creating in this Step-by-Step. The text to be entered is shown in bold here and in Figure 3-1.

   `<BR><A HREF="#FONTS">Fancy Fonts</A>`

3. As shown in Figure 3-1, add a new level 2 heading called **Fancy Fonts** just below the <HR> tag you created at the end of Step-by-Step 2.6 from Lesson 2 and just before the </BODY> tag. This will finish the internal hypertext link you started in step 2 of this Step-by-Step.

   `<P><H2><A NAME="FONTS">Fancy Fonts</A></H2></P>`

4. Below the new heading, near the end of your document, enter the font tags, attributes, and values exactly as shown here and in bold in Figure 3-1.

   ```
   <BR><FONT FACE=HELVETICA SIZE=4 COLOR=RED>This is the Helvetica font at Size 4</FONT>
   <BR><FONT FACE=TIMES SIZE=6 COLOR=GREEN>This is the Times font at Size 6</FONT>
   <BR><FONT FACE=ARIAL SIZE=8 COLOR=ORANGE>This is the Arial font at Size 8</FONT>
   <BR><FONT FACE=COURIER SIZE=2 COLOR=BLACK>This is the Courier font at Size 2</FONT>
   <HR>
   ```

Lesson 3 HTML Power Techniques

STEP-BY-STEP 3.1 Continued

5. Your tags should appear like those in Figure 3-1. Save your work as **fourteen.html** or **fourteen.htm**.

FIGURE 3-1
Applying font styles, sizes, and colors

```
<HTML>
<TITLE> HTML and JavaScript </TITLE>

<BODY BGCOLOR=WHITE TEXT=BLUE LINK=RED VLINK=GREEN>
<CENTER><H1>Organizing Tags</H1></CENTER>

<P>There are many ways to organize a Web page. This Web page will organize text, hypertext links, colors, and fonts. You'll also demonstrate single spacing, double spacing, and the use of line breaks. </P>

<P>This Web page will display how to organize Web pages in a number of ways using: </P>

<BR><A HREF="#POWERFUL">Powerful Lines</A>
<BR><A HREF="#HYPERLINKS">Hyperlinks to HTML and JavaScript Sources</A>
<BR><A HREF="#PREVIOUS">Hyperlinks to Previously Created Web Pages</A>
<BR><A HREF="#FONTS">Fancy Fonts</A>
<BR>Perfect Pictures
<BR>Orderly Tables
<BR>Extraordinary Extras

<HR>
<P><H2><A NAME="POWERFUL">Powerful Lines</A></H2></P>

A Horizontal Rule tag 50% wide and 10 pixels high.
<HR WIDTH=50% SIZE=10>

A Horizontal Rule tag 25% wide and 20 pixels high.
<HR WIDTH=25% SIZE=20>

A Horizontal Rule tag 10% wide and 30 pixels high.
<HR WIDTH=10% SIZE=30>

A Horizontal Rule tag without attributes and values.
<HR>

<P><H2><A NAME="HYPERLINKS">Hyperlinks to HTML and JavaScript Sources </A></H2></P>

<BR><A HREF="http://www.microsoft.com">Microsoft</A>
<BR><A HREF="http://home.netscape.com">Netscape</A>
<BR><A HREF="http://www.sun.com">Sun</A>
<BR><A HREF="http://www.oracle.com">Oracle</A>
<HR>
```

STEP-BY-STEP 3.1 Continued

FIGURE 3-1 (Continued)
Applying font styles, sizes, and colors

```
<P><H2><A NAME="PREVIOUS">Hyperlinks to Previously Created Web Pages
</A></H2></P>

<BR><A HREF="one.html">one</A>
<BR><A HREF="two.html">two</A>
<BR><A HREF="three.html">three</A>
<BR><A HREF="four.html">four</A>
<BR><A HREF="five.html">five</A>
<BR><A HREF="six.html">six</A>
<BR><A HREF="seven.html">seven</A>
<BR><A HREF="eight.html">eight</A>
<BR><A HREF="nine.html">nine</A>
<BR><A HREF="ten.html">ten</A>
<BR><A HREF="eleven.html">eleven</A>
<HR>

<P><H2><A NAME="FONTS">Fancy Fonts</A></H2></P>

<BR><FONT FACE=HELVETICA SIZE=4 COLOR=RED>This is the Helvetica font at Size 4</FONT>
<BR><FONT FACE=TIMES SIZE=6 COLOR=GREEN>This is the Times font at Size 6 </FONT>
<BR><FONT FACE=ARIAL SIZE=8 COLOR=ORANGE>This is the Arial font at Size 8 </FONT>
<BR><FONT FACE=COURIER SIZE=2 COLOR=BLACK>This is the Courier font at Size 2 </FONT>
<HR>

</BODY>
</HTML>
```

Lesson 3 HTML Power Techniques

HTML BASICS

STEP-BY-STEP 3.1 Continued

6. View your work in your Web browser. Your changes should look like Figure 3-2. Make any corrections that appear necessary.

FIGURE 3-2
Various font styles, sizes, and colors

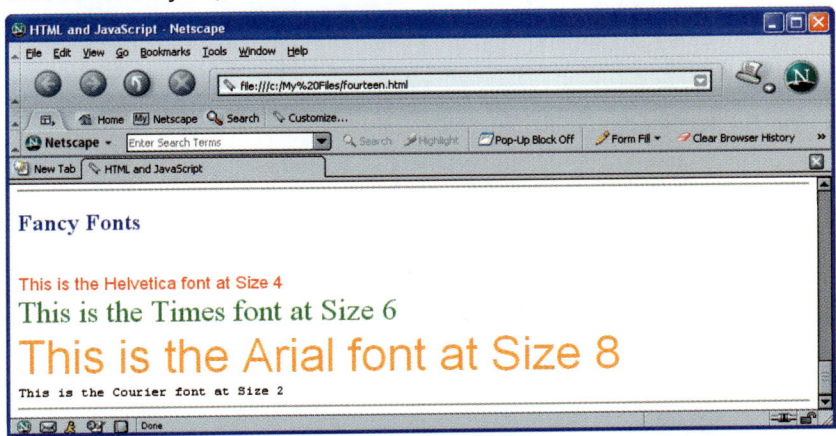

7. Continue to the next section or close your software and shut down your computer if you're finished for the day.

Downloading and Inserting Graphics

Pictures can be found in many places. You can find pictures in your clip art collection, scan pictures into your computer with a scanner, draw your own pictures, or copy them from the Web. However, before you can easily use pictures in your Web pages, you need to convert them into one of the acceptable Web formats. The common formats are .gif and .jpg or .jpeg.

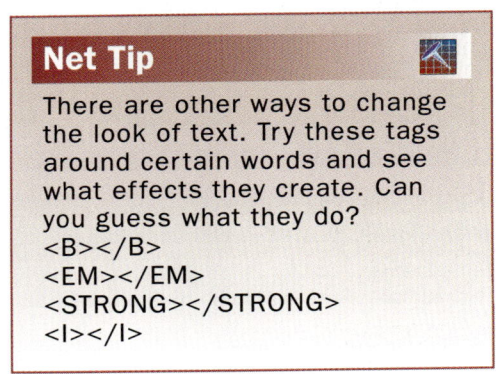

> **Net Tip**
> There are other ways to change the look of text. Try these tags around certain words and see what effects they create. Can you guess what they do?
> <B></B>
> <EM></EM>
> <STRONG></STRONG>
> <I></I>

The first type of graphics or image format, *.gif*, was originally created by one of the first online companies, CompuServe, to provide a compressed graphics format that could transfer easily over low-speed modems. The *Graphics Interchange Format* is usually abbreviated as GIF. There is some debate on how to say GIF. In some parts of the country it is pronounced with a hard *g* as in Kathie Lee GIFford. In other parts of the country it is pronounced with a soft *g* as in JIFfy Peanut Butter. Either pronunciation works. After all, the pronunciation doesn't change the file format in the least.

The second commonly used format is *.jpg* or *.jpeg*. It is pronounced *J-Peg* by Web artists in-the-know. JPEG is short for *Joint Photographic Experts Group*. This format adheres to an international set of graphics standards. JPEG graphics, like GIF pictures, are compact enough for Internet use.

68 HTML BASICS

Other graphic file formats are emerging. But if you know how to work with these two formats, you'll know how to work with any other picture format on the World Wide Web.

> **Net Tip**
>
> To copy and download the graphics you need for this lesson, go to *www.course.com*, search for the ISBN of this book, and follow the rest of the steps outlined in Step-by-Step 3.2. (The ISBN can be found on the back cover of the book.)

STEP-BY-STEP 3.2

1. Open your Web browser.

2. Enter the URL **www.course.com** in your Web browser.

3. Click in the Search For box as shown in Figure 3-3 and enter the ISBN of this book.

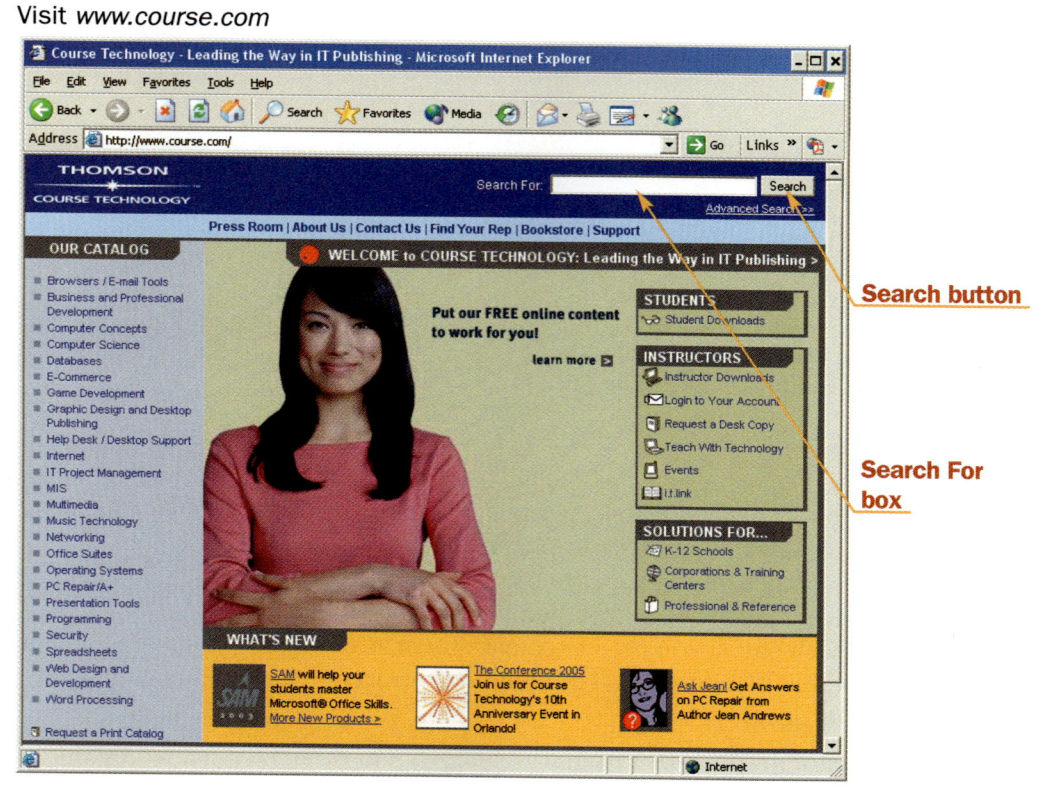

FIGURE 3-3
Visit *www.course.com*

4. Choose **Search** and wait for the results to appear.

5. Click on the title of this book, then choose the link called Student Online Companion.

6. Click the **Lesson 3** link and choose the **Data Files & Graphics** link from the list that appears. Scroll down until you see a dragon.

Lesson 3 HTML Power Techniques

HTML BASICS 69

STEP-BY-STEP 3.2 Continued

7. If you're on a Windows computer, click the right mouse button on the dragon's nose, pictured in Figure 3-4. If you're using a Macintosh, click and hold your mouse button on the dragon's nose.

   FIGURE 3-4
   Copy and save the graphic

   Right click in Windows

   Click and hold in Macintosh

8. Choose the **Save Image As...** or **Save Picture As...** command from the list that appears, as shown in Figures 3-5A and 3-5B. (*Note:* The command on your browser may be worded differently. Keep trying the various commands that appear until you find the correct command.)

   FIGURE 3-5A
   With Netscape, select Save Image

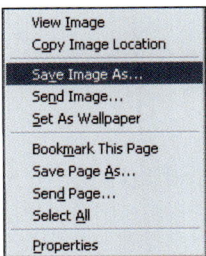

   FIGURE 3-5B
   With Internet Explorer, select Save Picture As

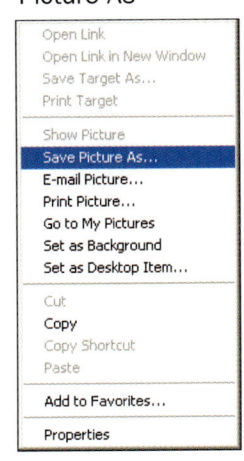

9. Save your file (called *levy.gif*) in the exact same folder where you have been saving your Web pages.

STEP-BY-STEP 3.2 Continued

10. Open your **fourteen.html** or **fourteen.htm** Web page in your word processor or text editor.

11. Create a hypertext link in the list near the top of the page that will hyperlink to the new section you will be creating. The text to be entered is shown in bold here and in Figure 3-6.

**
<A HREF="#PICTURES">Perfect Pictures</A>**

12. As shown in Figure 3-6, add a new level 2 heading called **Perfect Pictures** just below the last <HR> tag you created previously and just before the </BODY> tag. Include the <A NAME> tag so you can finish the internal hypertext link you started in step 11.

<P><H2><A NAME="PICTURES">Perfect Pictures</A></H2></P>

13. Below your new heading, near the end of your document, enter an Image Source <IMG SRC> tag, as shown here and in Figure 3-6. Notice that the name of the file you just downloaded appears between quotation marks.

<IMG SRC="levy.gif">
<HR>

14. Your tags should now appear like those in Figure 3-6. If everything looks correct, save your work as **fifteen.html** or **fifteen.htm**.

FIGURE 3-6
Inserting a graphic or image file

```
<HTML>
<TITLE> HTML and JavaScript </TITLE>

<BODY BGCOLOR=WHITE TEXT=BLUE LINK=RED VLINK=GREEN>
<CENTER><H1>Organizing Tags</H1></CENTER>

<P>There are many ways to organize a Web page. This Web page will organize text,
hypertext links, colors, and fonts. You'll also demonstrate single spacing, double spac-
ing, and the use of line breaks. </P>

<P>This Web page will display how to organize Web pages in a number of ways using: </P>

<BR><A HREF="#POWERFUL">Powerful Lines</A>
<BR><A HREF="#HYPERLINKS">Hyperlinks to HTML and JavaScript Sources</A>
<BR><A HREF="#PREVIOUS">Hyperlinks to Previously Created Web Pages</A>
<BR><A HREF="#FONTS">Fancy Fonts</A>
<BR><A HREF="#PICTURES">Perfect Pictures</A>
<BR>Orderly Tables
<BR>Extraordinary Extras

<HR>
<P><H2><A NAME="POWERFUL">Powerful Lines</A></H2></P>
A Horizontal Rule tag 50% wide and 10 pixels high.
<HR WIDTH=50% SIZE=10>
```

STEP-BY-STEP 3.2 Continued

FIGURE 3-6 (Continued)
Inserting a graphic or image file

```
A Horizontal Rule tag 25% wide and 20 pixels high.
<HR WIDTH=25% SIZE=20>

A Horizontal Rule tag 10% wide and 30 pixels high.
<HR WIDTH=10% SIZE=30>

A Horizontal Rule tag without attributes and values.
<HR>

<P><H2><A NAME="HYPERLINKS">Hyperlinks to HTML and JavaScript Sources
</A></H2></P>

<BR><A HREF="http://www.microsoft.com">Microsoft</A>
<BR><A HREF="http://home.netscape.com">Netscape</A>
<BR><A HREF="http://www.sun.com">Sun</A>
<BR><A HREF="http://www.oracle.com">Oracle</A>
<HR>

<P><H2><A NAME="PREVIOUS">Hyperlinks to Previously Created Web Pages
</A></H2></P>

<BR><A HREF="one.html">one</A>
<BR><A HREF="two.html">two</A>
<BR><A HREF="three.html">three</A>
<BR><A HREF="four.html">four</A>
<BR><A HREF="five.html">five</A>
<BR><A HREF="six.html">six</A>
<BR><A HREF="seven.html">seven</A>
<BR><A HREF="eight.html">eight</A>
<BR><A HREF="nine.html">nine</A>
<BR><A HREF="ten.html">ten</A>
<BR><A HREF="eleven.html">eleven</A>
<HR>

<P><H2><A NAME="FONTS">Fancy Fonts</A></H2></P>

<BR><FONT FACE=HELVETICA SIZE=4 COLOR=RED>This is the Helvetica font at Size 4</FONT>
<BR><FONT FACE=TIMES SIZE=6 COLOR=GREEN>This is the Times font at Size 6 </FONT>
<BR><FONT FACE=ARIAL SIZE=8 COLOR=ORANGE>This is the Arial font at Size 8 </FONT>
<BR><FONT FACE=COURIER SIZE=2 COLOR=BLACK>This is the Courier font at Size 2 </FONT>
<HR>
```

STEP-BY-STEP 3.2 Continued

FIGURE 3-6 (Continued)
Inserting a graphic or image file

```
<P><H2><A NAME="PICTURES">Perfect Pictures</A></H2></P>

<IMG SRC="levy.gif">
<HR>

</BODY>
</HTML>
```

15. View your work in your Web browser. Your picture should look like Figure 3-7, but it may appear larger or smaller in your browser.

FIGURE 3-7
Your GIF image as seen in a browser

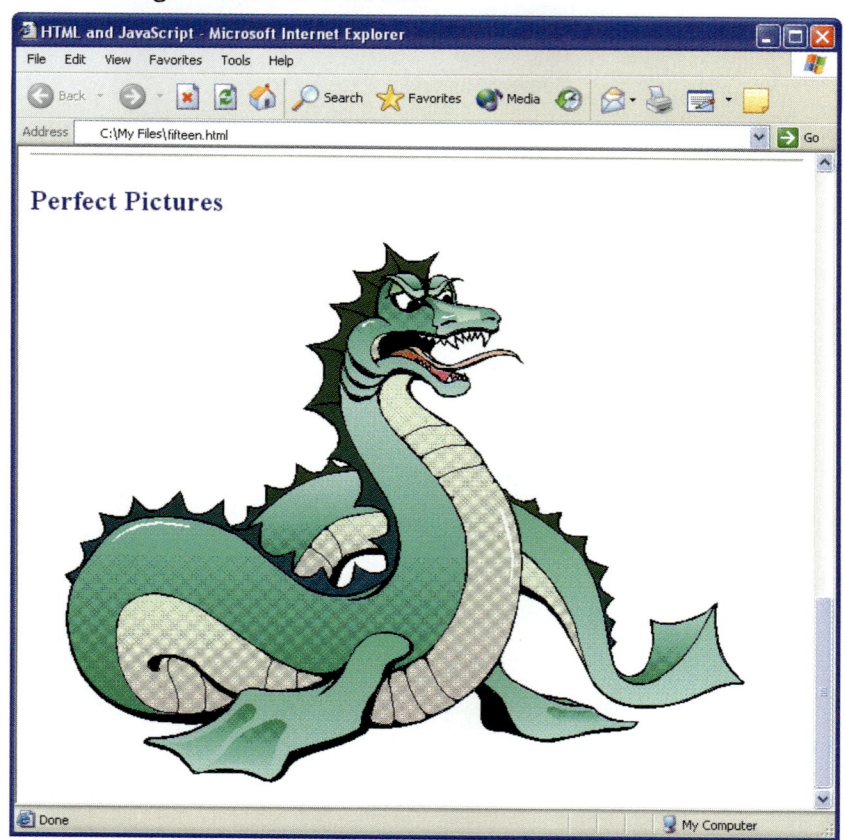

16. Continue to the next section or close your software and shut down your computer if you're finished for the day.

Pictures of All Sizes

Pictures can be altered in a variety of ways by changing a tag's values. Pictures can be used as wallpaper to cover the entire background of a Web page. They can be aligned in the center, to the left side, or to the right side of a page. They can be made bigger or smaller, depending on your needs.

You can also change the size of the picture by using the HEIGHT and WIDTH attributes. Controlling the exact size of a picture can be very helpful in making a page look sharp and interesting.

In the first part of Step-by-Step 3.3, you'll align your picture to the right of the page and make it small. In the second section, you'll align three dragons of varying sizes across the page, and then you'll place three dragons vertically on the Web page by manipulating a few tags.

> **Net Tip**
>
> A common error is created by transposing the R and the C in the <IMG SRC> tag. Think of this as the IMaGe SouRCe tag and you won't forget to place the letters in the right order.

> **Net Tip**
>
> An easy way to allow your Web page visitors to e-mail you with one click is to create the following tag:
> <A HREF=mailto:your_email@address>Your Name</A>.

STEP-BY-STEP 3.3

1. Open your **fifteen.html** or **fifteen.htm** file for text editing.

2. Near the end of your document, add the following information to your <IMG SRC> tag as shown in bold here and in Figure 3-8.

   <P><IMG SRC="levy.gif" **ALIGN=RIGHT HEIGHT=50 WIDTH=50**></P>

Technology Careers

Artists on the Web

Artists are in great demand among Web site development companies. There was a time when a Web page would be made entirely of words or text. Today, pictures dominate Web pages, attracting a greater number of visitors than ever before.

If you are considering an artistic career, consider the Web. You may find that much of your artwork will end up on the Web. Big corporations with Web sites and Web site developers are always on the lookout for great artists.

You can create your art using any medium or method you like. Scanners can convert your pictures into digital images. Digital files can be converted into formats that will work on the Web such as .gif or .jpg. You can also use a variety of art software to create your works of art or to improve any art you have scanned into Web images.

The best training for a Web artist would be to take as many art classes as you can. The graphics tools you need to use to convert your artwork are easily learned. The skills of an artist will take much more time to develop.

STEP-BY-STEP 3.3 Continued

3. Save your changes as **sixteen.html** or **sixteen.htm**.

4. View your changes in your Web browser. The dragon should appear smaller and right-aligned as shown in Figure 3-9.

5. Next, create three images that appear across the screen, with each graphic appearing as a different size. To do so, enter the following tags below your first IMG SRC tag, as shown here and in Figure 3-8.

```
<IMG SRC="levy.gif" HEIGHT=100 WIDTH=100>
<IMG SRC="levy.gif" HEIGHT=150 WIDTH=150>
<IMG SRC="levy.gif" HEIGHT=200 WIDTH=200>
```

6. Resave your changes using the same **sixteen.html** or **sixteen.htm** filename and view your additions in your Web browser. Your changes should appear similar to the three images shown in Figure 3-9. If your graphics don't appear, make any necessary corrections, resave, and view again.

7. Just below the three tags you entered in the previous step, add two more IMG SRC tags, using <P> tags to cause several graphics to appear vertically. Enter these tags exactly as shown here and in Figure 3-8.

```
<P><IMG SRC="levy.gif" HEIGHT=150 WIDTH=150></P>
<P><IMG SRC="levy.gif" HEIGHT=200 WIDTH=200></P>
```

8. Save your changes again as **sixteen.html** or **sixteen.htm**, and view the result in your Web browser. Check Figures 3-8 and 3-9 to evaluate how the tags and graphics should appear. Make corrections where necessary, and review any changes in your browser.

9. Continue to the next section or close your software and shut down your computer if you're finished for the day.

FIGURE 3-8
Dragons everywhere

```
<HTML>
<TITLE> HTML and JavaScript </TITLE>

<BODY BGCOLOR=WHITE TEXT=BLUE LINK=RED VLINK=GREEN>
<CENTER><H1>Organizing Tags</H1></CENTER>

<P>There are many ways to organize a Web page. This Web page will organize text, hypertext links, colors, and fonts. You'll also demonstrate single spacing, double spacing, and the use of line breaks. </P>

<P>This Web page will display how to organize Web pages in a number of ways using: </P>

<BR><A HREF="#POWERFUL">Powerful Lines</A>
<BR><A HREF="#HYPERLINKS">Hyperlinks to HTML and JavaScript Sources</A>
```

Lesson 3 HTML Power Techniques

STEP-BY-STEP 3.3 Continued

FIGURE 3-8 (Continued)
Dragons everywhere

```
<BR><A HREF="#PREVIOUS">Hyperlinks to Previously Created Web Pages</A>
<BR><A HREF="#FONTS">Fancy Fonts</A>
<BR><A HREF="#PICTURES">Perfect Pictures</A>
<BR>Orderly Tables
<BR>Extraordinary Extras

<HR>
<P><H2><A NAME="POWERFUL">Powerful Lines</A></H2></P>

A Horizontal Rule tag 50% wide and 10 pixels high.
<HR WIDTH=50% SIZE=10>

A Horizontal Rule tag 25% wide and 20 pixels high.
<HR WIDTH=25% SIZE=20>

A Horizontal Rule tag 10% wide and 30 pixels high.
<HR WIDTH=10% SIZE=30>

A Horizontal Rule tag without attributes and values.
<HR>

<P><H2><A NAME="HYPERLINKS">Hyperlinks to HTML and JavaScript Sources</A></H2></P>

<BR><A HREF="http://www.microsoft.com">Microsoft</A>
<BR><A HREF="http://home.netscape.com">Netscape</A>
<BR><A HREF="http://www.sun.com">Sun</A>
<BR><A HREF="http://www.oracle.com">Oracle</A>
<HR>

<P><H2><A NAME="PREVIOUS">Hyperlinks to Previously Created Web Pages</A></H2></P>

<BR><A HREF="one.html">one</A>
<BR><A HREF="two.html">two</A>
<BR><A HREF="three.html">three</A>
<BR><A HREF="four.html">four</A>
<BR><A HREF="five.html">five</A>
<BR><A HREF="six.html">six</A>
<BR><A HREF="seven.html">seven</A>
<BR><A HREF="eight.html">eight</A>
<BR><A HREF="nine.html">nine</A>
<BR><A HREF="ten.html">ten</A>
<BR><A HREF="eleven.html">eleven</A>
<HR>
```

STEP-BY-STEP 3.3 Continued

FIGURE 3-8 (Continued)
Dragons everywhere

```
<P><H2><A NAME="FONTS">Fancy Fonts</A></H2></P>

<BR><FONT FACE=HELVETICA SIZE=4 COLOR=RED>This is the Helvetica font at Size 4</FONT>
<BR><FONT FACE=TIMES SIZE=6 COLOR=GREEN>This is the Times font at Size 6 </FONT>
<BR><FONT FACE=ARIAL SIZE=8 COLOR=ORANGE>This is the Arial font at Size 8 </FONT>
<BR><FONT FACE=COURIER SIZE=2 COLOR=BLACK>This is the Courier font at Size 2 </FONT>
<HR>

<P><H2><A NAME="PICTURES">Perfect Pictures</A></H2></P>

<P><IMG SRC="levy.gif" ALIGN=RIGHT HEIGHT=50 WIDTH=50></P>

<IMG SRC="levy.gif" HEIGHT=100 WIDTH=100>
<IMG SRC="levy.gif" HEIGHT=150 WIDTH=150>
<IMG SRC="levy.gif" HEIGHT=200 WIDTH=200>

<P><IMG SRC="levy.gif" HEIGHT=150 WIDTH=150></P>
<P><IMG SRC="levy.gif" HEIGHT=200 WIDTH=200></P>
<HR>

</BODY>
</HTML>
```

Net Ethics

Picture Piracy

One of the big problems on the Web is picture piracy. Since it is so easy to pull pictures off the Web, many people do so without permission. Many pictures are copyrighted; that is, someone owns them. To use them, you need to obtain permission or pay the owner or the artist.

For instance, Disney has many copyrighted images. They have taken legal action against Web site creators who grab and illegally use or alter Disney's copyrighted images.

Consider which pictures you download and use from the Web. Are they free for you to use? Many places allow the free download of images. For instance, the images you borrowed from the Web site for this book are authorized for your use.

Lesson 3 HTML Power Techniques

HTML BASICS 77

STEP-BY-STEP 3.3 Continued

FIGURE 3-9
Your GIF images after changing their attributes and values

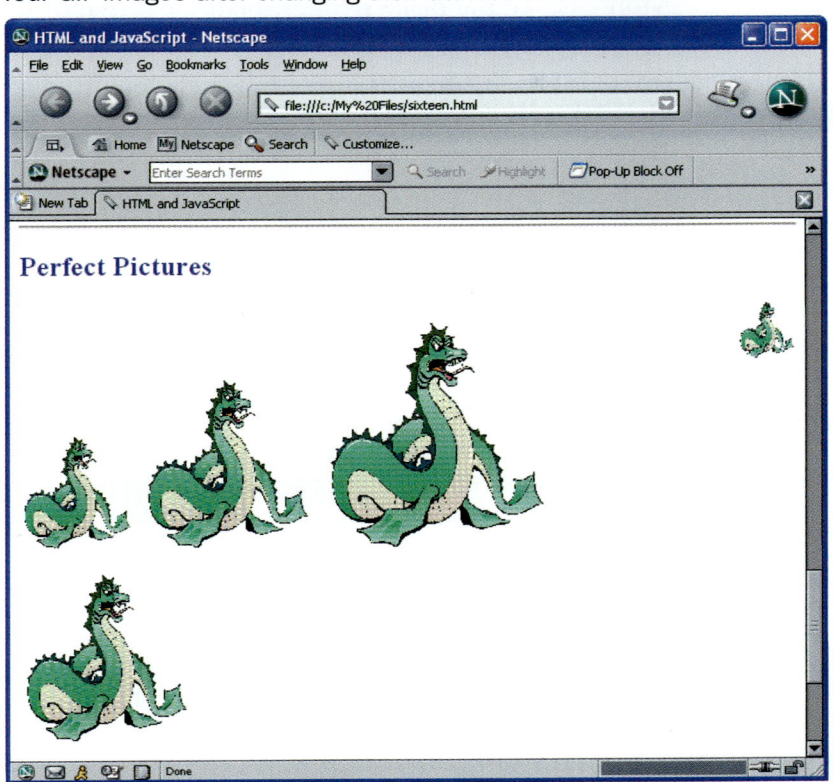

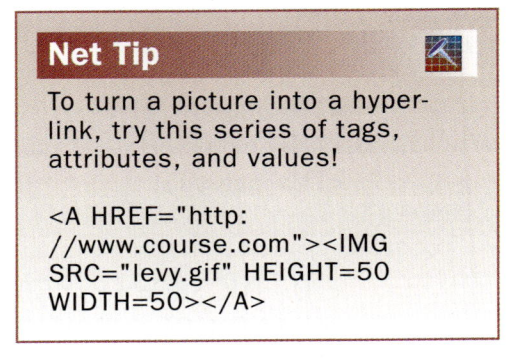

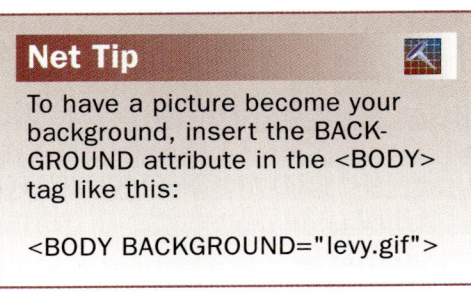

Net Tip

To turn a picture into a hyperlink, try this series of tags, attributes, and values!

`<A HREF="http://www.course.com"><IMG SRC="levy.gif" HEIGHT=50 WIDTH=50></A>`

Net Tip

To have a picture become your background, insert the BACKGROUND attribute in the <BODY> tag like this:

`<BODY BACKGROUND="levy.gif">`

Orderly Tables

When you think of a dining room table, well-set and ready for a big holiday dinner, you think of how organized everything is. All the place settings, plates, cups, and silverware are well ordered and in just the right spots.

Electronic tables are like that. Tables create little boxes in which you can place things to keep them organized. In Step-by-Step 3.4, you will create a table and then insert many of the tags you have already learned into little boxes called *table cells*.

Creating a table is so easy with the <TABLE> tag. A cell can have a border by adding a BORDER attribute and a number value. You can also make cells appear larger around pictures and text with the CELLPADDING attribute. Within cells, you can align pictures and text to the center, left, or right.

STEP-BY-STEP 3.4

1. Open your **sixteen.html** or **sixteen.htm** file, if necessary.

2. Create a hypertext link in your listing at the top of the page that will hyperlink to the new section you are creating. The text to be entered is shown in bold here and in Figure 3-10.

<A HREF="#TABLES">Orderly Tables</A>

3. As shown in Figure 3-10, add a new level 2 heading called **Orderly Tables** just below the <HR> tag you created in the previous Step-by-Step and just before the </BODY> tag. Include the <A NAME> tag so you can complete the internal hyperlinks you started in Step 2.

   <P><H2><A NAME="TABLES">Orderly Tables</A></H2></P>

4. Below the new heading, near the end of your document, enter the <TABLE> tags, attributes, and values, exactly as shown here and in bold in Figure 3-10.

```
<TABLE BORDER=5 CELLPADDING=10 ALIGN=CENTER>
<TR>
        <TH>Dragons</TH>
        <TH>Colors</TH>
        <TH>Fonts</TH>
</TR>
<TR>
        <TD><IMG SRC="LEVY.GIF" HEIGHT=50 WIDTH=50></TD>
        <TD BGCOLOR=RED ALIGN=CENTER>Red</TD>
        <TD ALIGN=CENTER><FONT FACE=TIMES SIZE=7 COLOR=GREEN>Times</TD>
</TR>
<TR>
        <TD><IMG SRC="LEVY.GIF" HEIGHT=75 WIDTH=50></TD>
        <TD BGCOLOR=GREEN ALIGN=CENTER>Green</TD>
        <TD ALIGN=CENTER><FONT FACE=COURIER SIZE=10 COLOR=GREEN>Courier</TD>
</TR>
</TABLE>
<HR>
```

Lesson 3 HTML Power Techniques

HTML BASICS

STEP-BY-STEP 3.4 Continued

5. Your tags should now appear like those in Figure 3-10. Save your work as **seventeen.html** or **seventeen.htm**.

FIGURE 3-10
Creating a table in HTML

```
<HTML>
<TITLE> HTML and JavaScript </TITLE>

<BODY BGCOLOR=WHITE TEXT=BLUE LINK=RED VLINK=GREEN>
<CENTER><H1>Organizing Tags</H1></CENTER>

<P>There are many ways to organize a Web page.  This Web page will organize text,
hypertext links, colors, and fonts.  You'll also demonstrate single spacing, double spac-
ing, and the use of line breaks. </P>

<P>This Web page will display how to organize Web pages in a number of ways using: </P>

<BR><A HREF="#POWERFUL">Powerful Lines</A>
<BR><A HREF="#HYPERLINKS">Hyperlinks to HTML and JavaScript Sources</A>
<BR><A HREF="#PREVIOUS">Hyperlinks to Previously Created Web Pages</A>
<BR><A HREF="#FONTS">Fancy Fonts</A>
<BR><A HREF="#PICTURES">Perfect Pictures</A>
<BR><A HREF="#TABLES">Orderly Tables</A>
<BR>Extraordinary Extras

<HR>
<P><H2><A NAME="POWERFUL">Powerful Lines</A></H2></P>

A Horizontal Rule tag 50% wide and 10 pixels high.
<HR WIDTH=50% SIZE=10>

A Horizontal Rule tag 25% wide and 20 pixels high.
<HR WIDTH=25% SIZE=20>

A Horizontal Rule tag 10% wide and 30 pixels high.
<HR WIDTH=10% SIZE=30>

A Horizontal Rule tag without attributes and values.
<HR>

<P><H2><A NAME="HYPERLINKS">Hyperlinks to HTML and JavaScript Sources
</A></H2></P>

<BR><A HREF="http://www.microsoft.com">Microsoft</A>
<BR><A HREF="http://home.netscape.com">Netscape</A>
<BR><A HREF="http://www.sun.com">Sun</A>
```

STEP-BY-STEP 3.4 Continued

FIGURE 3-10 (Continued)
Creating a table in HTML

```
<BR><A HREF="http://www.oracle.com">Oracle</A>
<HR>

<P><H2><A NAME="PREVIOUS">Hyperlinks to Previously Created Web Pages
</A></H2></P>

<BR><A HREF="one.html">one</A>
<BR><A HREF="two.html">two</A>
<BR><A HREF="three.html">three</A>
<BR><A HREF="four.html">four</A>
<BR><A HREF="five.html">five</A>
<BR><A HREF="six.html">six</A>
<BR><A HREF="seven.html">seven</A>
<BR><A HREF="eight.html">eight</A>
<BR><A HREF="nine.html">nine</A>
<BR><A HREF="ten.html">ten</A>
<BR><A HREF="eleven.html">eleven</A>
<HR>

<P><H2><A NAME="FONTS">Fancy Fonts</A></H2></P>

<BR><FONT FACE=HELVETICA SIZE=4 COLOR=RED>This is the Helvetica font at Size 4</FONT>
<BR><FONT FACE=TIMES SIZE=6 COLOR=GREEN>This is the Times font at Size 6 </FONT>
<BR><FONT FACE=ARIAL SIZE=8 COLOR=ORANGE>This is the Arial font at Size 8 </FONT>
<BR><FONT FACE=COURIER SIZE=2 COLOR=BLACK>This is the Courier font at Size 2 </FONT>
<HR>

<P><H2><A NAME="PICTURES">Perfect Pictures</A></H2></P>

<P><IMG SRC="levy.gif" ALIGN=RIGHT HEIGHT=50 WIDTH=50></P>

<IMG SRC="levy.gif" HEIGHT=100 WIDTH=100>
<IMG SRC="levy.gif" HEIGHT=150 WIDTH=150>
<IMG SRC="levy.gif" HEIGHT=200 WIDTH=200>

<P><IMG SRC="levy.gif" HEIGHT=150 WIDTH=150></P>
<P><IMG SRC="levy.gif" HEIGHT=200 WIDTH=200></P>
<HR>

<P><H2><A NAME="TABLES">Orderly Tables</A></H2></P>
```

Lesson 3 HTML Power Techniques

HTML BASICS 81

STEP-BY-STEP 3.4 Continued

FIGURE 3-10 (Continued)
Creating a table in HTML

```
<TABLE BORDER=5 CELLPADDING=10 ALIGN=CENTER>
<TR>
        <TH>Dragons</TH>
        <TH>Colors</TH>
        <TH>Fonts</TH>
</TR>
<TR>
        <TD><IMG SRC="LEVY.GIF" HEIGHT=50 WIDTH=50></TD>
        <TD BGCOLOR=RED ALIGN=CENTER>Red</TD>
        <TD ALIGN=CENTER><FONT FACE=TIMES SIZE=7
        COLOR=GREEN>Times</TD>
</TR>
<TR>
        <TD><IMG SRC="LEVY.GIF" HEIGHT=75 WIDTH=50></TD>
        <TD BGCOLOR=GREEN ALIGN=CENTER>Green</TD>
        <TD ALIGN=CENTER><FONT FACE=COURIER SIZE=10
        COLOR=GREEN>Courier</TD>
</TR>
</TABLE>
<HR>

</BODY>
</HTML>
```

STEP-BY-STEP 3.4 Continued

6. View your work in your Web browser. Your new page should look like Figure 3-11. Make any corrections that are necessary.

FIGURE 3-11
An HTML table as seen in your browser

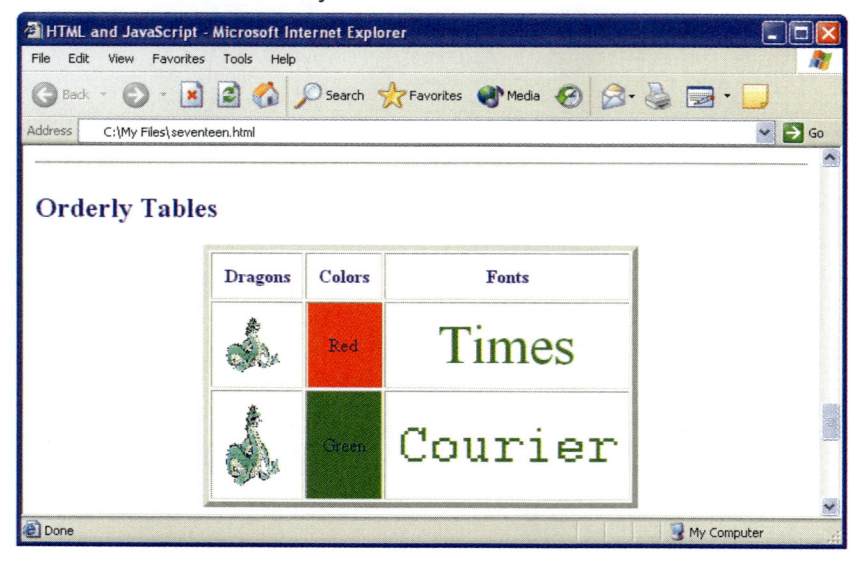

7. Continue to the next section or close your software and shut down your computer if you're finished for the day.

Internet Milestone

Business on the Web

For many years, the Web was a tough place to make a living. The truth is, it took many years before the commercial potential of the Web was realized. Some of the first Web companies to start making a considerable profit online were America Online, Yahoo!, and Amazon.com.

Some succeeded online by daring to go where no one else dared to go. Many said that the Web would never replace bookstores. The people of Amazon.com took exception to that theory and began selling books on the Web. They sold so many books that other book companies quickly realized that they had to go online or give away a big portion of their business to Amazon.com. Barnes & Noble was one of the first major booksellers to join Amazon.com on the WWW.

Sony discovered that the Web was a great place to sell music CDs. Egghead.com, a leading electronics company, found the Web a great place to sell software. What other kinds of things can you think of that could become big sellers online? Can you set up a cyberbusiness and make lots of money from the Web?

Extraordinary Extras

In Step-by-Step 3.5, you'll learn a few extra tags that add extraordinary power to your Web pages. These tags will allow those who visit your Web page to interact with the document.

Many data input or <FORM> tag options have been added to HTML. These options give you many ways to ask questions of visitors to your Web page. These tags give extra functionality to your Web page and can make your Web page more exciting and extraordinary.

You will use the following four basic input tags throughout these lessons:

- *Text box* – A box where Web site visitors can dictate or key responses.
- *Drop-down list* – Displays an option and a special arrow symbol that allows users to view other possible responses.
- *Radio button* – Sometimes referred to as an option button, allows you to choose one option from a group of options.
- *Check box* – A box that places a check mark in its center when a user selects an option from a group.

As you work through this last Step-by-Step activity of this lesson, think about how you should integrate the new tags into your Web page. Don't worry; you'll pass with flying font colors! If you have any questions, review the steps in previous activities. Figure 3-12 on the next page displays the new tags you will be adding to your Web page.

FIGURE 3-12
A variety of data input tags

```
<FORM>

Enter your first name:
<INPUT TYPE="TEXT" SIZE="25">
<BR>
Enter your last name:
<INPUT TYPE="TEXT" SIZE="25">
<P>

<SELECT>
<OPTION SELECTED>Pick your favorite team from the list:
<OPTION>Chicago Bulls
<OPTION>Utah Jazz
<OPTION>Los Angeles Lakers
<OPTION>Indiana Pacers
<OPTION>New Jersey Nets
<OPTION>Phoenix Suns
</SELECT>
<P>

The best place to eat is:
<BR>
<INPUT TYPE="RADIO" NAME="BEST">Wendy's<BR>
<INPUT TYPE="RADIO" NAME="BEST">McDonald's<BR>
<INPUT TYPE="RADIO" NAME="BEST">Taco Bell<BR>
<INPUT TYPE="RADIO" NAME="BEST">Burger King<BR>
<INPUT TYPE="RADIO" NAME="BEST">Kentucky Fried Chicken<BR>
<P>

I like to eat:
<BR>
<INPUT TYPE="CHECKBOX">Hamburgers<BR>
<INPUT TYPE="CHECKBOX">Tacos<BR>
<INPUT TYPE="CHECKBOX">Chicken Strips<BR>
<INPUT TYPE="CHECKBOX">Fries<BR>
<INPUT TYPE="CHECKBOX">Hot Dogs<BR>
<P>

</FORM>
<HR>
```

Lesson 3 HTML Power Techniques

STEP-BY-STEP 3.5

1. Open your **seventeen.html** or **seventeen.htm** file, if necessary.

2. Create a section near the end of your Web page called **Extraordinary Extras**.

3. Create an internal hypertext link in the index list near the top of your Web page that will link to the new section you are creating. Call this link **Extraordinary Extras**.

4. Change the color, font size, and font face of the title of your new section in any way you see fit.

5. Enter the tags shown in Figure 3-12 in your new Extraordinary Extras section, just after the last <HR> tag and before the </BODY> tag at the bottom of the page.

6. Save your work as **eighteen.html** or **eighteen.htm**.

7. Open your Web browser and try all the input options. They should appear like those found in Figure 3-13. Which ones work? Correct any errors you find, resave, and try them again.

FIGURE 3-13
Extraordinary Extras created with Forms

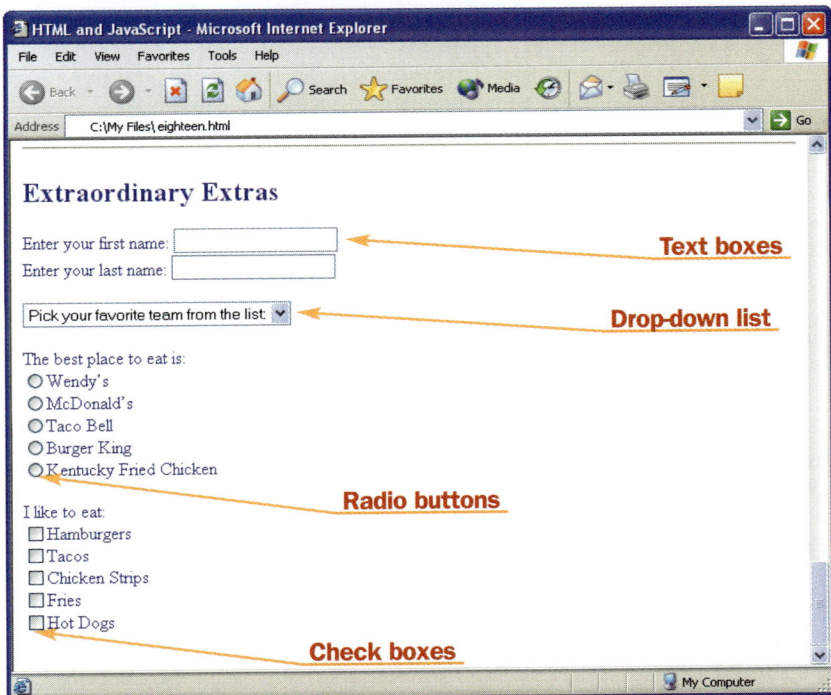

8. Modify your form options. Return to your Web page and change all the selection items.

9. Save your work as **eighteen-2.html** or **eighteen-2.htm** and test your changes. How did they work?

10. Continue to the Summary section, or close your software and shut down your computer if you're finished for the day.

SUMMARY

In this lesson, you learned:

- You can control the size, style, and color of fonts.
- You can download pictures from the Web.
- You can insert pictures into your Web pages.
- You can change the size of graphics.
- You can use tables to organize information.
- You can turn pictures into hyperlinks.
- You can insert a variety of data input options into a Web page.

> **Net Tip**
>
> It is considered impolite to download pictures to your school network that you don't intend to use. Graphics take up a great deal of space on a computer. Downloading hundreds and hundreds of pictures and not using them is a waste of network server drive space. Consider deleting any pictures you aren't actually using.

VOCABULARY Review

Define the following terms:

| .gif | Graphics Interchange Format | Table cells |
| .jpg or .jpeg | Joint Photographic Experts Group | |

REVIEW Questions

TRUE/FALSE

Circle T if the statement is true or F if the statement is false.

T F 1. You can only change the color of a font with attributes and values placed in the <BODY> tag.

T F 2. You can make an image as big or small as you like.

T F 3. GIF stands for Greater Image Format.

T F 4. All images are available for you to use free over the Internet.

T F 5. The CELLPADDING attribute makes the area between your table cells larger or smaller.

Lesson 3 HTML Power Techniques

FILL IN THE BLANK

Complete the following sentences by writing the correct word or words in the blanks provided.

1. You can use _____ tags to place pictures and text in an orderly fashion on a Web page.
2. _____ tags allow you to collect information about people who visit your site.
3. The _____ image format was created by CompuServe.
4. The _____ tag creates an item in a drop-down list in a form.
5. The _____ image format is an international standard.

WRITTEN QUESTIONS

Write a brief answer to the following questions.

1. Why are artists in such demand on the WWW?

2. When is it illegal to take pictures off the Web?

3. Why is it important not to download pictures to your school or workplace network if you do not plan to use them?

4. How and why would you use the following tags or attributes?

    <B></B>

    <EM></EM>

<STRONG></STRONG>

<I></I>

<ALIGN=CENTER>

5. What tags would you use to insert a graphic or a hyperlink?

PROJECTS

PROJECT 3-1

GreatApplications, Inc., wants to enter the online videogame business. However, before it starts programming the next great online videogame, it wants to survey potential customers to see what kinds of online games they want to play and buy.

Brainstorm 10 questions that will help GreatApplications, Inc., learn what its customers want in a videogame program. Using your <FORM> tag skills, create an online survey to gather information from potential customers, such as the respondents' names and e-mail addresses. Ask questions that utilize drop-down lists, radio selection items, and check boxes.

TEAMWORK PROJECT

GreatApplications, Inc., is asking your team to plan a world tour to demonstrate its new software videogames to people in five major cities. Your team has been asked to create a calendar of events for the tour using <TABLE> tags. The tour must be conducted during a single month and should involve five major cities.

When you create your calendar, create links to tourist information about the cities that you will be visiting on the tour. Use cellpadding and cell borders to make the table interesting. You can even put pictures in the cells to illustrate the five cities you have selected for the software rollout.

Lesson 3 HTML Power Techniques

WEB PROJECT

How fast can you substitute the levy.gif graphic for another graphic? Think about another graphic you like. How could you manipulate the attributes and values to display your new graphic in a variety of sizes? Go for it! Make the changes! Save your changed file as **web-project.html** or **web-project.htm**.

CRITICAL *Thinking*

ACTIVITY 3-1

Prepare a 100- to 250-word answer to each of the following questions.

1. How important is the WWW and HTML to the world's economy? What makes them so important?
2. How can the Web benefit small businesses, such as a family-owned flower shop, a local antique store, or a fancy hair salon?
3. Over 500 years ago, Johannes Gutenberg invented movable type, which lead to an explosion in the amount of printed material available to common people and changed the history of the world. But what about 500 years from now? How will people look back on the invention of HTML?

ACTIVITY 3-2

Prepare a 100- to 250-word answer to each of the following questions.

1. Other than changing font size, what can you do with fonts to make your Web pages more interesting?
2. How can tables be used to display information in your HTML pages? What kinds of things can you create with table tags?
3. What extra features or tags would you like to see added to HTML? What tags do you think should be added to give more power to HTML?

ACTIVITY 3-3

Each of these extraordinary input boxes asks the user to supply a different kind of information. What kinds of responses would you expect from the following FORM attributes?

TEXT

OPTION

RADIO

CHECKBOX

SUMMARY *Project*

The local city zoo has hired you to create a Web page that describes some of the animals they currently have on display. They want your Web page to be well organized they also want you to include images of the animals along with a short descriptive paragraph about each. Use the information you learned in this lesson about tables, fonts, and images to complete this assignment. When you are finished, your Web page should look something like the one shown in Figure 3-14 below.

FIGURE 3-14
A sample Web page for the local city zoo

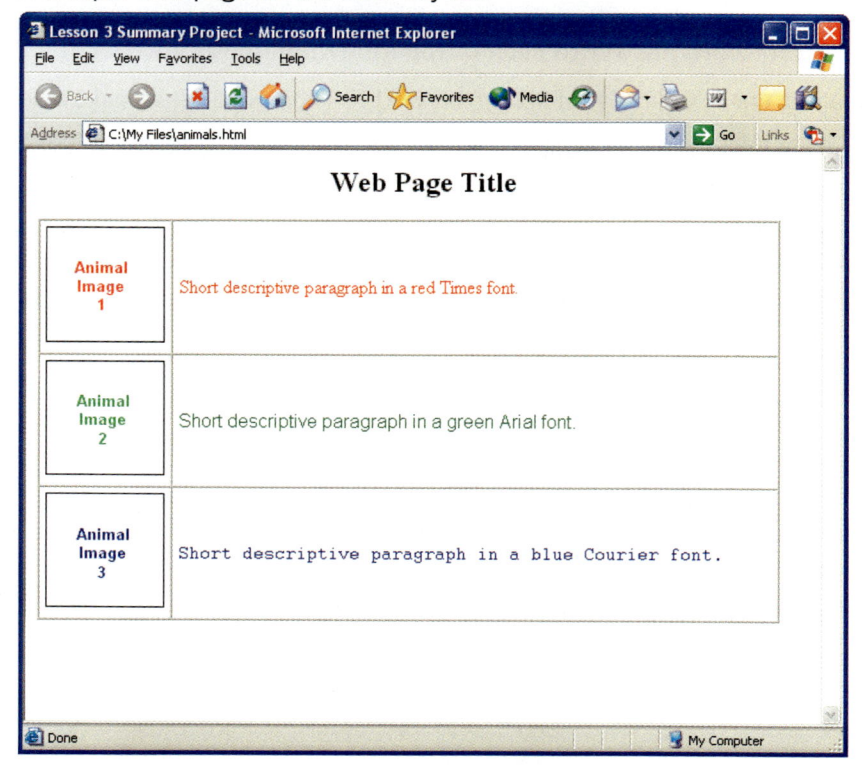

Project Requirements

- Your Web page should have an appropriate title at the top.
- Your animal images should be kept to an appropriate size within the Web page.
- The descriptive paragraph for each animal should be displayed in a variety of font faces and colors.
- The paragraphs should be about 500 pixels wide.
- Your table should have a visible border that separates each cell.

Net Tip

Probably the best way for you to find animal images to use in your page is to surf the Web. Once you have found an animal picture that you want to use, follow the instructions in this lesson to download the image to your workstation. Keep in mind, however, that it is inappropriate for you to download copyrighted images from the Web. Please avoid using any image that displays a copyright message on it or on the Web page where it is located.

LESSON 4

HTML Structural Design Techniques

OBJECTIVES

Upon completion of this lesson, you should be able to:

- Create a frame set.
- Add a navigation bar.
- Make a welcome page.
- Create a nested frame set.
- Include a title bar frame and page.
- Utilize frame and frame set options.

Estimated Time: 1.5 hrs.

VOCABULARY

Frames
Frame set tag
Left-hand navigation
Navigation bar
Nested frame set
Pixel
Title bar

Creating an HTML Frame Set

In Lesson 2 you learned how to make your Web browser link from one Web page to another page through the use of hyperlinks. Now it is time to learn how to make your Web browser display two or more Web pages on the screen at the same time! The HTML tags that will help you accomplish this are the <FRAMESET> tag and the <FRAME> tag.

As its name implies, the *frame set tag* allows you to define a set of rectangular areas on your screen called *frames* (see Figure 4-1). Each frame is capable of displaying a different Web page. In a way, you can make your Web browser behave as though you had multiple browsers running on your computer at the same time. However, a frame set allows a Web page in one frame to communicate with a page in a different frame. You'll learn more about this concept later in this lesson.

FIGURE 4-1
Three frames on a Web page

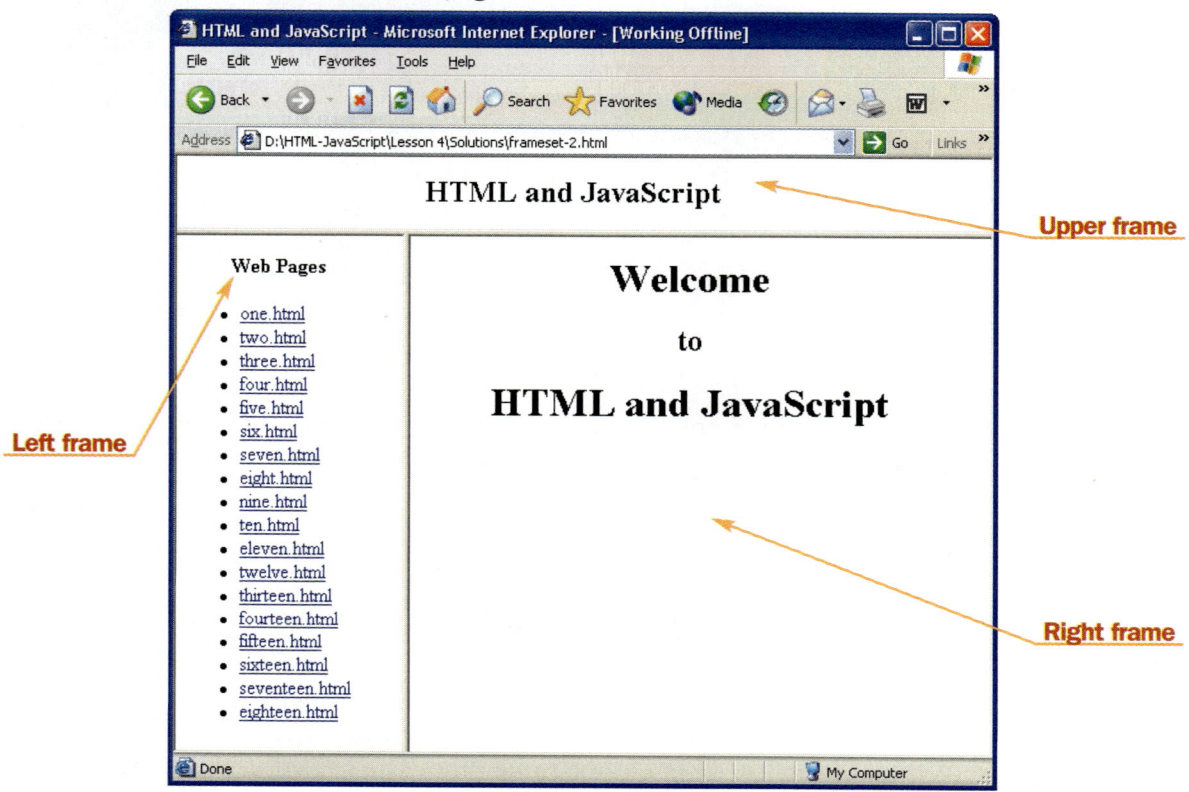

When you create your first HTML frame set file you will notice that it has many things in common with the other HTML pages you created in the previous lessons. However, you should also recognize an important difference. Specifically, you will see that a frame set page does not contain the familiar <BODY> and </BODY> tags that are such an important part of standard Web pages. Instead, the frame set page will contain <FRAMESET> and </FRAMESET> tags that mark the beginning and the end of the frame definition.

In addition, the frame set tag can contain a ROWS attribute or a COLS attribute. The purpose of the ROWS attribute is to give you the means to define horizontal frames, and to specify the height of each frame. Similarly, the COLS attribute allows you to create vertical frames, and to designate the width of each frame. Since you can define only horizontal or vertical frames within any given frame set, the <FRAMESET> tag may contain a ROWS attribute or a COLS attribute, but not both.

As you will see in the following Step-by-Step, the frame set tags will encapsulate two or more <FRAME> tags. In turn, the <FRAME> tags will contain at least two important attributes called NAME and SRC that allow you to give each frame a name, and to specify the source Web page that you wish to have displayed in each frame, respectively. The purpose of the SRC (source) attribute is quite obvious, but the function of the NAME attribute is not immediately apparent. Don't worry. You will learn more about this attribute in Step-by-Step 4.4.

Lesson 4 HTML Structural Design Techniques

STEP-BY-STEP 4.1

1. Open Notepad, SimpleText, or your favorite text editor.
2. Enter the HTML text exactly as shown in Figure 4-2.

> **Important**
>
> As you have already learned, you can save files with either an .htm or .html extension. Be careful! If you have used the .htm extension, you must change all the file names in Figure 4-2 accordingly. For example, change navbar.html to navbar.htm in the frame set file.

> **Note**
>
> The asterisk (*) means "whatever's left."

FIGURE 4-2
Name a text file with an .html extension

```
<HTML>
<TITLE>HTML and JavaScript</TITLE>

<FRAMESET COLS="180,*">
<FRAME NAME="LeftFrame" SRC="navbar.html">
<FRAME NAME="RightFrame" SRC="welcome.html">
</FRAMESET>
</HTML>
```

3. Save your newly created file as **frameset-1.html** or **frameset-1.htm**. Proceed to the next Step-by-Step section or close down your system if you are finished for today.

> **Important**
>
> The numbers that accompany the ROWS and COLS attributes can be absolute *pixel* values or percentage values. A pixel is an individual tiny dot of light inside a computer monitor or screen. In step 2 you made the frame set column 180 pixels of light wide. There are thousands of pixels on a typical computer screen, too many to count. Therefore, it's sometimes easier to calculate the percentage values of a screen instead of counting pixels. A percentage value will automatically calculate the 5%, 10%, 50% or more of a screen when deciding how much of the screen to dedicate to a frame. For example,
> <FRAMESET COLS="20%,*">.

Creating a Navigation Bar

One design that is very commonly used by professional Web designers is to place a Web page in a narrow left-hand frame that contains many hyperlinks. When the user clicks on any of these links, the appropriate Web page is displayed in the larger right-hand frame. This design technique is often referred to as *left-hand navigation*, and the Web page containing the hyperlinks is called a navigation bar. A *navigation bar* is a series of hyperlinks, usually organized horizontally or vertically on a Web page or in a frame. It is used to navigate a Web site. Figure 4-3 shows an example of a Web page with a navigation bar.

FIGURE 4-3
Two frames and a navigation bar on a Web page

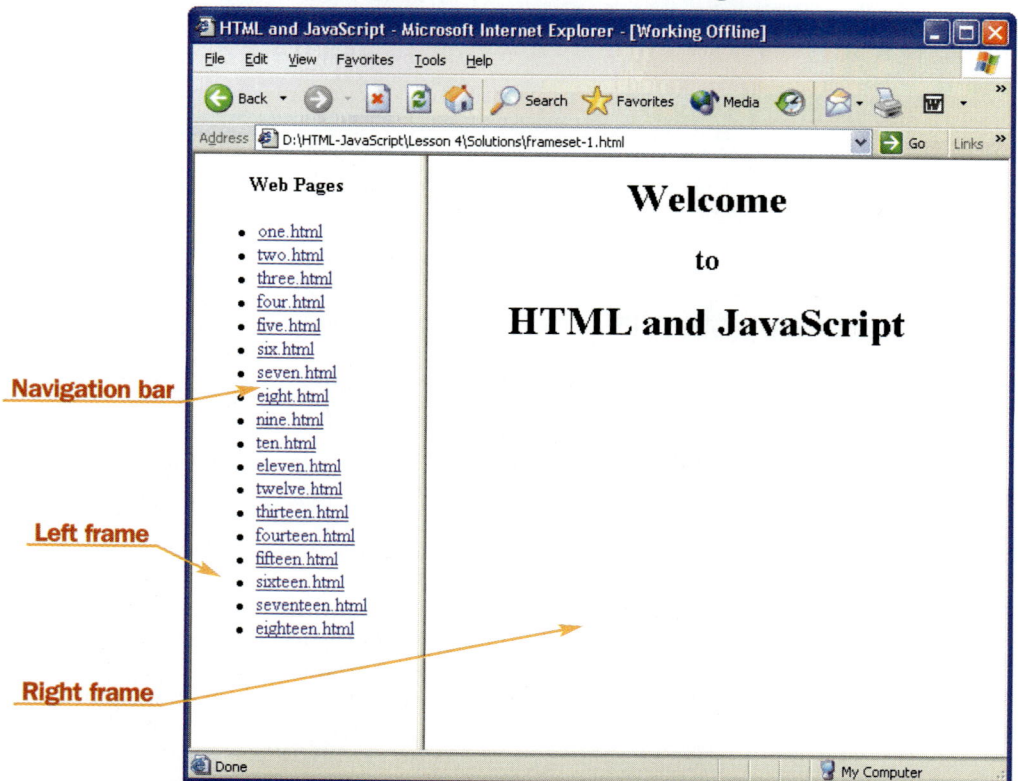

At this point in the lesson, we will show you how to create your own navigation bar and to make use of the previous eighteen Web pages you created in Lessons 1, 2, and 3. Your navigation bar will contain an unordered list of eighteen hyperlinks, and these links will refer to the Web pages you previously saved as one.html, two.html, three.html, etc.

The HTML tags you will use to create your navigation bar are not anything special. In fact, they are all tags that you have already used in previous lessons. However, you will see a new attribute in the <A> tag that defines the hyperlinks to the Web pages that will be displayed in the right-hand frame. This attribute is called TARGET, and its purpose is to tell the browser which frame it should use to display the target Web page. You should also take note of the fact that the TARGET attribute uses the frame name that you defined with the NAME attribute in the <FRAME> tag in Step-by-Step 4.1.

Lesson 4 HTML Structural Design Techniques

STEP-BY-STEP 4.2

1. Open Notepad, SimpleText, or your favorite text editor if it is not already open.

2. Enter the HTML text exactly as shown in Figure 4-4.

FIGURE 4-4
Navigation tags in a frames page

```
<HTML>
<TITLE>HTML and JavaScript</TITLE>

<BODY>
<CENTER><B>Web Pages</B></CENTER>
<UL>
<LI><A HREF="one.html" TARGET="RightFrame">one.html</A></LI>
<LI><A HREF="two.html" TARGET="RightFrame">two.html</A></LI>
<LI><A HREF="three.html" TARGET="RightFrame">three.html</A></LI>
<LI><A HREF="four.html" TARGET="RightFrame">four.html</A></LI>
<LI><A HREF="five.html" TARGET="RightFrame">five.html</A></LI>
<LI><A HREF="six.html" TARGET="RightFrame">six.html</A></LI>
<LI><A HREF="seven.html" TARGET="RightFrame">seven.html</A></LI>
<LI><A HREF="eight.html" TARGET="RightFrame">eight.html</A></LI>
<LI><A HREF="nine.html" TARGET="RightFrame">nine.html</A></LI>
<LI><A HREF="ten.html" TARGET="RightFrame">ten.html</A></LI>
<LI><A HREF="eleven.html" TARGET="RightFrame">eleven.html</A></LI>
<LI><A HREF="twelve.html" TARGET="RightFrame">twelve.html</A></LI>
<LI><A HREF="thirteen.html" TARGET="RightFrame">thirteen.html</A></LI>
<LI><A HREF="fourteen.html" TARGET="RightFrame">fourteen.html</A></LI>
<LI><A HREF="fifteen.html" TARGET="RightFrame">fifteen.html</A></LI>
<LI><A HREF="sixteen.html" TARGET="RightFrame">sixteen.html</A></LI>
<LI><A HREF="seventeen.html" TARGET="RightFrame">seventeen.html</A></LI>
<LI><A HREF="eighteen.html" TARGET="RightFrame">eighteen.html</A></LI>
</UL>
</BODY>

</HTML>
```

3. Save your newly created file as **navbar.html** or **navbar.htm**.

4. Proceed to the next Step-by-Step section in order to learn how to create a Web site welcome page or close down your system if your are finished for today.

> **Net Tip**
>
> Normally when a user clicks on a hyperlink, the target Web page will be loaded into the same frame as the link. The TARGET attribute overrides this behavior and sends the proper Web page to the "target" frame.

Creating a Web Site Welcome Page

Normally a professional Web site developer will create a welcome page that users will see when they first access the site. As you learned in Lesson 1, the primary purpose of the welcome page is simply to give users a good first impression of the site, and to ensure that they recognize the purpose of the site. For example, a company that wants to sell books, music, or other products over the Web wants to create a fancy welcome page that will catch the users' eyes, emphasize the company name, and allow easy access to the various parts of the Web site.

In this next Step-by-Step section you will create a very simple welcome page. In fact, there will be no HTML tags in this page that you have not already seen in earlier lessons. But you should recognize the fact that this page has a particular purpose, and could be enhanced dramatically to liven up your Web site and give the user a memorable experience. One of the primary goals of commercial Web sites is to give users a reason to return to the site again and again.

STEP-BY-STEP 4.3

1. Open Notepad, SimpleText, or your favorite text editor if it is not already open.

2. Enter the HTML text exactly as shown in Figure 4-5.

FIGURE 4-5
Create a simple welcome page

```
<HTML>
<TITLE>HTML and JavaScript</TITLE>

<BODY>
<CENTER><FONT SIZE=6><B>Welcome</B></FONT></CENTER>
<BR>
<CENTER><FONT SIZE=5><B>to</B></FONT></CENTER>
<BR>
<CENTER><FONT SIZE=6><B>HTML and JavaScript</B></FONT></CENTER>
</BODY>

</HTML>
```

3. Save your newly created file as **welcome.html** or **welcome.htm**.

Lesson 4 HTML Structural Design Techniques

HTML BASICS

STEP-BY-STEP 4.3 Continued

4. Open your Web browser and view the frameset-1.html document you created in Step-by-Step 4.1. You should see something much like Figure 4-6.

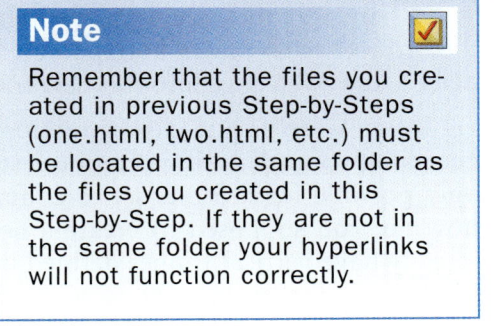

> **Note**
>
> Remember that the files you created in previous Step-by-Steps (one.html, two.html, etc.) must be located in the same folder as the files you created in this Step-by-Step. If they are not in the same folder your hyperlinks will not function correctly.

FIGURE 4-6
A welcome page with a navigation bar

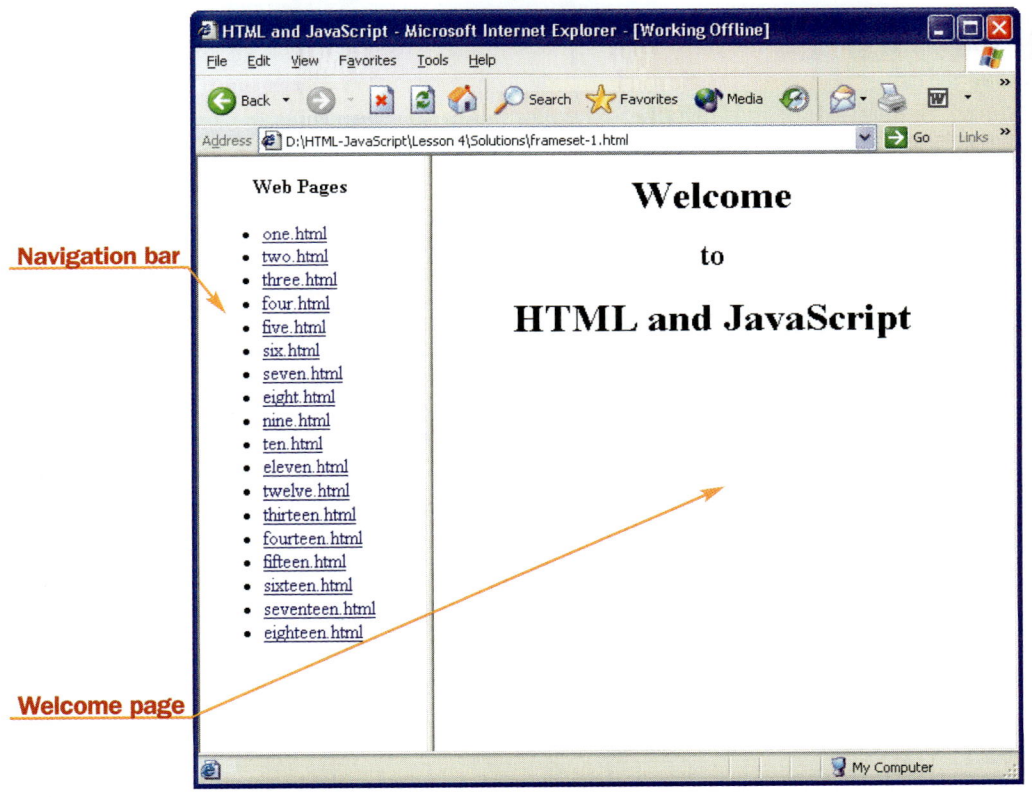

5. Proceed to the next Step-by-Step section in order to learn how to create a nested frame set, or close down your system if you are finished for today.

Creating a Nested Frame Set

There are times when it is desirable to place a third frame into your frame set that will cause the browser to display a horizontal frame across the top of your browser window. You may then place a new Web page into this new frame that could function as a constant title for your Web site.

If you were paying close attention to the material in the first part of this lesson, you should be asking yourself an important question about now. To be specific, we stated early on that it is only possible for a frame set to contain horizontal frames or vertical frames, but not both. So how are you supposed to create a horizontal frame in which to display your title page if you already have vertical frames defined in your existing frame set?

A *nested frame set* solves this problem. The term *nested* is a word that programmers and Web developers use to describe a structure, keyword, or tag that contains one or more additional instances of the same item. In this case, you will use a <FRAMESET> tag inside of another <FRAMESET> tag in order to create both vertical and horizontal frames.

STEP-BY-STEP 4.4

1. Open Notepad, SimpleText, or your favorite text editor if it is not already open.

2. Retrieve the **frameset-1.html** or **frameset-1.htm** file you created in Step-by-Step 4.1.

3. Modify the HTML document by adding the text in bold shown in Figure 4-7 below.

FIGURE 4-7
Name a text file with an .html extension

```
<HTML>
<TITLE>HTML and JavaScript</TITLE>

<FRAMESET ROWS="60,*">
<FRAME NAME="UpperFrame" SRC="title.html">

<FRAMESET COLS="180,*">
<FRAME NAME="LeftFrame" SRC="navbar.html">
<FRAME NAME="RightFrame" SRC="welcome.html">
</FRAMESET>

</FRAMESET>
</HTML>
```

4. Save your newly created file as **frameset-2.html** or **frameset-2.htm**.

5. Proceed to the next section to create a title page for your nested page, or close your system if you are finished for today.

Lesson 4 HTML Structural Design Techniques   HTML BASICS   99

Creating a Title Bar

Just as the Web page you created in Step-by-Step 4.2 is referred to as a navigation bar, a page that has the specific purpose of displaying a constant title for a Web site is commonly called a *title bar*. In this section you will create a title bar to be displayed in the new frame you defined in the previous exercise. Figure 4-8 shows an example of a Web page with a title bar.

FIGURE 4-8
Three frames with a navigation bar, title bar, and welcome page

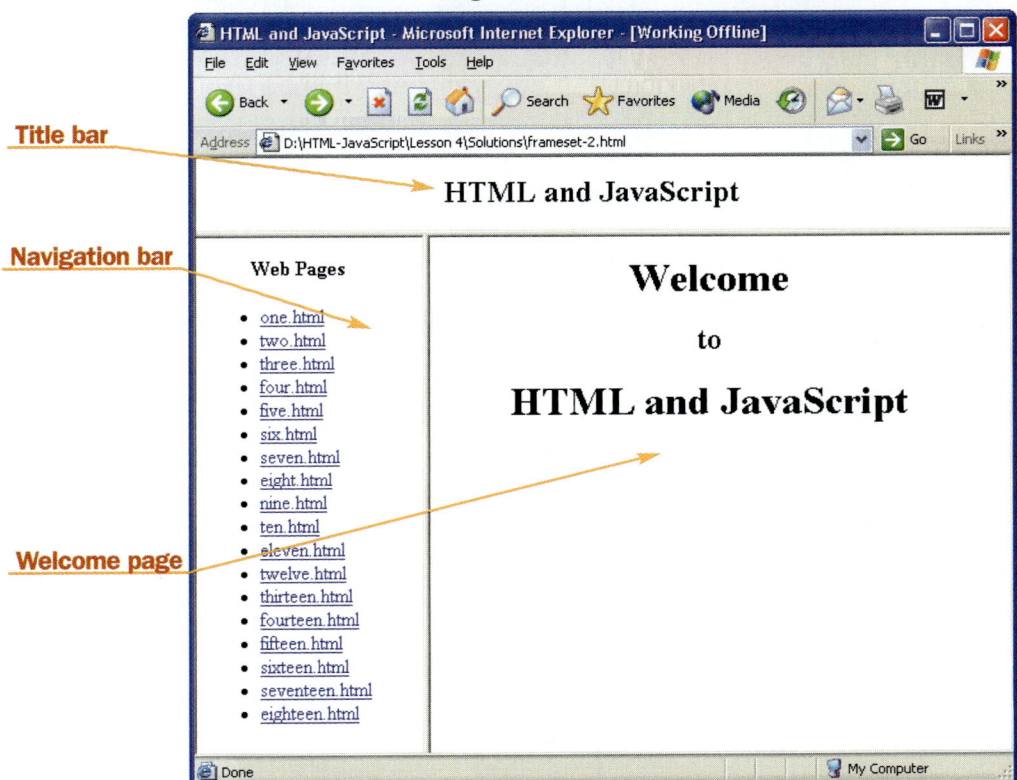

Like the welcome.html or welcome.htm page you created in Step-by-Step 4.3, this title bar Web page will not contain any new HTML tags. But, as with welcome pages, professional Web developers will typically go to great lengths to create a title bar that will be eye-catching and memorable. Yours, however, will be very simple so that you can more easily grasp this new concept.

STEP-BY-STEP 4.5

1. Open Notepad, SimpleText, or your favorite text editor if it is not already open.

STEP-BY-STEP 4.5 Continued

2. Enter the HTML text exactly as shown in Figure 4-9.

FIGURE 4-9
Tags for a title page

```
<HTML>
<TITLE>HTML and JavaScript</TITLE>

<BODY>
<CENTER><FONT SIZE=5><B>HTML and JavaScript</B></FONT></CENTER>
</BODY>

</HTML>
```

3. Save your newly created file as **title.html** or **title.htm**.

4. Open your Web browser and view the **frameset-2.html** or **frameset-2.htm** document you created in Step-by-Step 4.4. You should see a page like Figure 4-10.

STEP-BY-STEP 4.5 Continued

5. Frame pages can be customized by the user. Slowly roll your mouse over the bars (called frame separators) between the frames as marked in Figure 4-10. When a double arrow appears, click and drag the bar to the left or right or up and down.

FIGURE 4-10
Drag frame separators to customize a page

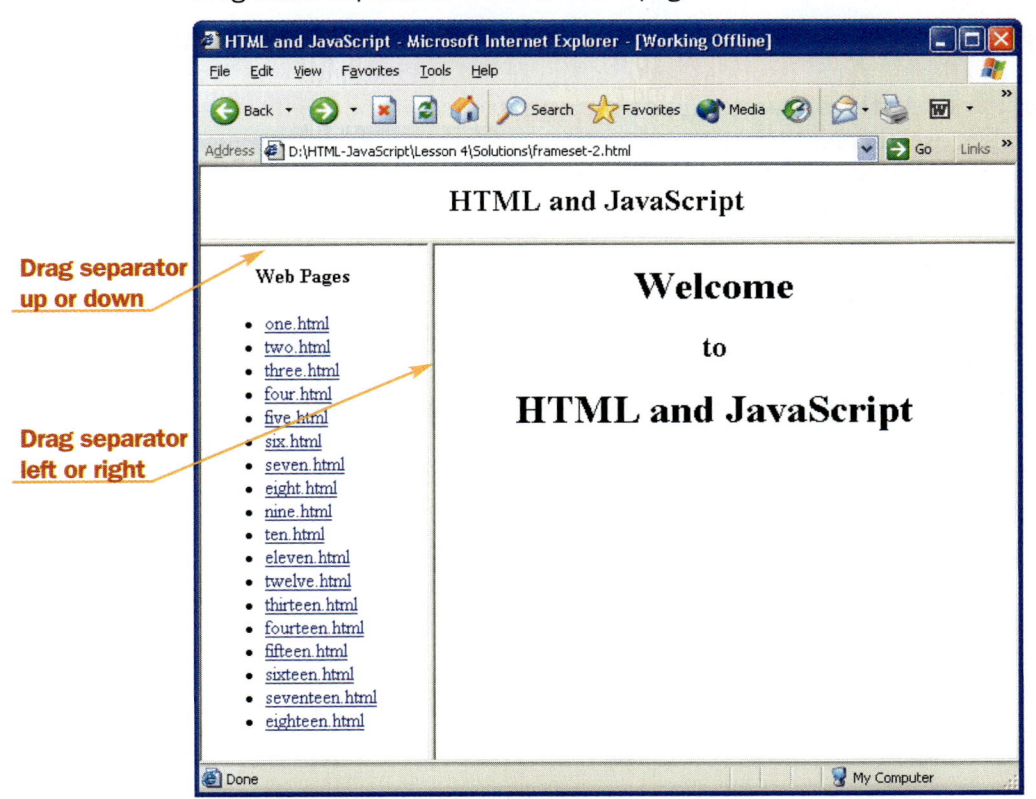

6. Proceed to the next section or close your system if you are finished for today.

> **Net Tip**
>
> Frames are a great way to learn how Web pages can be organized into sections or parts. Tables provide another way to split a page into sections for artistic and organizational purposes.

Using Advanced HTML Options

Let's take a minute to make a couple of observations about the frames and frame sets you have created so far. First of all, your Web browser is displaying frame separators that make it abundantly obvious where one frame ends and where another frame begins. Secondly, if you position your mouse cursor directly over any one of these frame separators, you will see your mouse pointer change shape to indicate that the frame separator may be moved. This means the user can change the appearance of your Web pages simply by clicking and dragging a frame separator to a different position, as you experienced in the previous exercise.

The frame and frame set characteristics we have just described may be desirable in some situations. However, there are many occasions when professional Web developers do not want the browser to display frame separators, nor would they want the user to be able to change the layout of the screen at will. This is especially true when the developer includes custom-made graphic images in their Web pages. Such images are frequently designed to be a specific size and to fit within a frame of an exact size. If the browser displays frame separators, or if the user were to change the size of the frames, the entire layout of the page could be disrupted, and the resulting clutter of images would be very unappealing.

Fortunately, two important HTML attributes may be used with the <FRAMESET> and <FRAME> tags to address these issues as seen in Figure 4-11. First, you may use the BORDER attribute within the FRAMESET tag to adjust the appearance of the frame separators. In addition, you may also use the NORESIZE attribute within the <FRAME> tags to instruct the browser that the user should not be able to change the size of the frames. These two attributes may be used separately or together to get the appearance and behavior you want.

FIGURE 4-11
Eliminate frame separators on a page

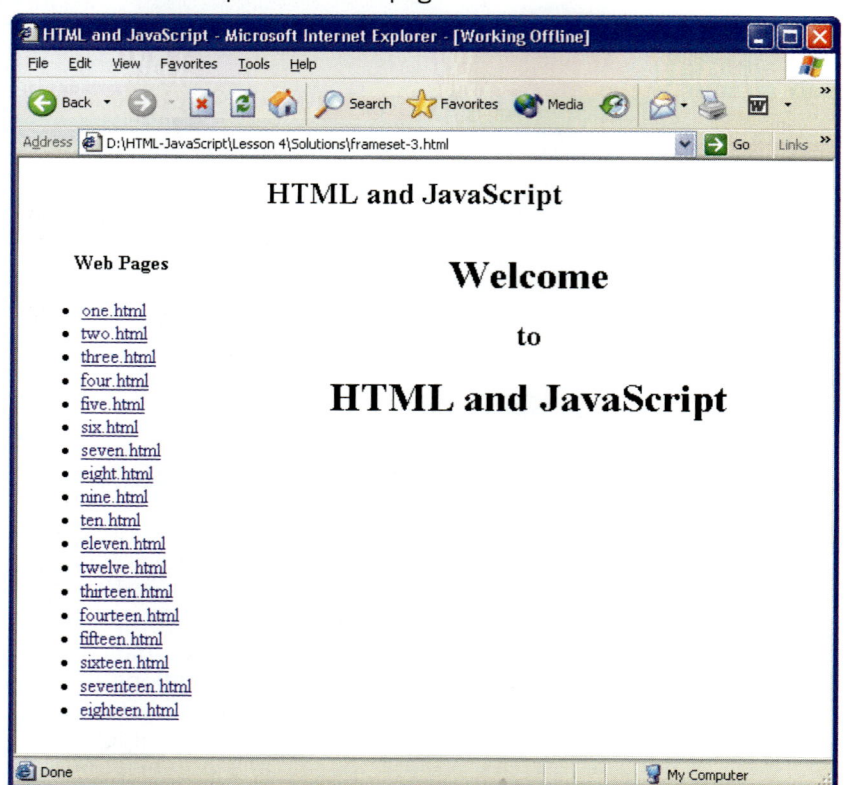

STEP-BY-STEP 4.6

1. Open Notepad, SimpleText, or your favorite text editor if it is not already open.

2. Retrieve the **frameset-2.html** or **frameset-2.htm** file you created in Step-by-Step 4.4.

STEP-BY-STEP 4.6 Continued

3. Modify the HTML document by adding the bold text shown in Figure 4-12 below.

FIGURE 4-12
Adding to a text file with an .html extension

```
<HTML>
<TITLE>HTML and JavaScript</TITLE>

<FRAMESET BORDER=0 ROWS="60,*">
<FRAME NAME="UpperFrame" NORESIZE SRC="title.html">

<FRAMESET BORDER=0 COLS="180,*">
<FRAME NAME="LeftFrame" NORESIZE SRC="navbar.html">
<FRAME NAME="RightFrame" NORESIZE SRC="welcome.html">
</FRAMESET>

</FRAMESET>
</HTML>
```

4. Save your newly created file as **frameset-3.html** or **frameset-3.htm**.

5. Open your Web browser and view the frameset-3.html document you just saved. You should see something much like Figure 4-11.

6. Proceed to the Summary section or close your system if you are finished for today.

FIGURE 4-13
HTML tags in Dreamweaver

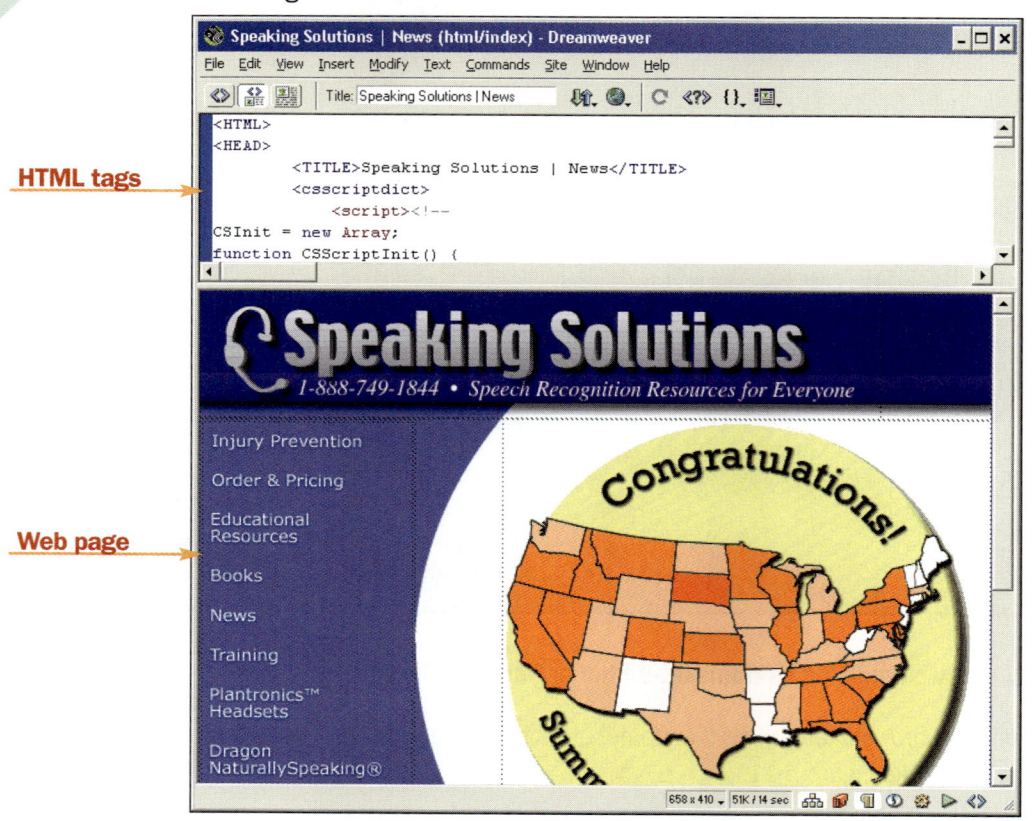

HTML tags →
Web page →

Internet Milestone

HTML Creation Tools

HTML is powerful, but it can take forever to enter all the tags by hand. Someone finally asked, "Is there any way to make HTML simpler to create?" A few years after HTML became the standard way of communicating online, enterprising programmers created software tools that take the pain out of typing in all of the angle brackets and tags. Some of the most popular Web page development tools include Macromedia Dreamweaver, Adobe GoLive, and Microsoft FrontPage. Each of these tools helps you create Web pages in much the same way professionals create documents in word processing or desktop publishing software.

In a program like Dreamweaver, most of the tags will be created for you automatically as you design a page. However, don't believe for a minute that you won't need to know HTML tags to use these powerful and exciting Web page creation tools! There will be times when you will need to edit or make corrections to the tags created by these products. A tag view is always available.

For instance, Figure 4-13 shows a Web page being created using Dreamweaver. Notice that in the bottom portion of the screen you can see the Web page much as it will appear online. However, in the top portion of the Dreamweaver tool you can still view the tags. Knowing how the tags work will help you become an expert Dreamweaver Web page developer and editor.

Lesson 4 HTML Structural Design Techniques   HTML BASICS   105

SUMMARY

In this lesson, you learned:

- You can create a frame set.
- You can interpret frame set attributes and values.
- You can create a navigation bar in a frame.
- You can make a simple welcome page for a frames page.
- You can insert nested tags and attributes.
- You can insert a title bar frame on a Web page.

VOCABULARY *Review*

Define the following terms:

Frames	Navigation bar	Pixel
Frame set tag	Nested frame set	Title bar
Left-hand navigation		

REVIEW *Questions*

TRUE/FALSE

Circle T if the statement is true or F if the statement is false.

T F 1. A frame set can display either rows or columns.

T F 2. The <BODY> tag can be omitted from a frame set page.

T F 3. You must hand-key tags when you use programs like FrontPage, Dreamweaver, or GoLive.

T F 4. The only way to calculate the width of a frame is to count pixels.

T F 5. The TARGET attribute makes frame separators disappear.

FILL IN THE BLANK

Complete the following sentences by writing the correct word or words in the blanks provided.

1. The _____ attribute points a Web page to display in a specific frame.
2. The _____ attribute creates vertically separated frames.
3. The _____ attribute creates horizontally separated frames.

4. The _____ =0 attribute makes frame separators disappear.

5. The _____ attribute prevents viewers of a Web page from changing the size of frames.

WRITTEN QUESTIONS

Write a brief answer to the following questions.

1. What is the purpose of a welcome page as described in this lesson?

2. What is left-hand navigation? Explain how to create a left-hand navigation bar.

3. What is nesting from a programmer's perspective as described in this lesson?

4. What are pixel values and percentage values, and how are they defined in terms of a frame set?

5. Why would a Web site developer want to prevent visitors to the Web site from adjusting the row and column separators on a frames page?

PROJECTS

PROJECT 4-1

In Project 1-1, you used your Web searching skills to locate information on HTML, HTML guides, and about learning HTML. Your manager has asked that you organize the information you collected into a new frames Web page using two columns only.

GreatApplications, Inc. has asked you to create a Web site with left-hand navigation that will organize the information you collected in Project 1-1 and Table 1-2. This way these helpful Web pages can be made available to everyone in the company online. Create a navigation frame on the left-hand side of your frame set page, and have the information you are linking to appear in the right-hand frame. You can do all of this with tags you have learned in this text.

TEAMWORK PROJECT

In this teamwork project, you are to conduct a survey. To complete the survey you and your team members must visit at least 100 different Web sites. With teamwork, this won't be as difficult as it may first appear. In the Teamwork Project in Lesson 1, you identified the greatest Web pages you could find. In Critical Thinking Activity 2-2, you organized pages you like for easy reference in a Web page that you saved as My Web Resources. In PROJECT 2-1 you identified the five worst pages you could find on the Web. Between all the members of your team you must have already visited over 100 sites.

As a team, revisit both the best and the worst pages you have listed. Visit other sites if necessary. You must, as a team, survey exactly 100 sites, collecting data as you go. Divide the task with each member taking a certain percentage of the sites to view while recording the results of applying the following questions to each Web site.

Survey Questions

1. Investigate. Viewing the source HTML code of your 100 Web pages, how many use frame tags or some type of frame organization to organize their Web pages?

2. Calculate. Viewing the source of your Web pages, how many of these pages use table tags to organize their Web pages?

3. Tabulate. What percentage of these good and bad sites use left-hand navigation systems?

4. Record. How many of the sites use navigation systems at the top of the Web page?

5. How many of these Web sites use an attractive graphic or logo in the title bar area at the top of the Web page?

6. What percentage of the Web sites visited, in the opinion of your team members, have effective welcome pages?

WEB PROJECT

In Project 4-1, you created a left-hand navigation system that will allow you to share with your colleagues at GreatApplications, Inc. information about HTML. In this Web Project, challenge yourself. Change the Web page you created in Project 4-1 to a site that navigates from the top bar of the page. Create two rows in your frame set. In the top frame, create your navigation system using 20 percent of the screen. In the bottom frame, display the information. Save this project as WebProject-4.html or WebProject-4.htm.

CRITICAL *Thinking*

SCANS **ACTIVITY 4-1**

In your opinion, what are the top ten most important things you have learned about HTML and creating Web pages while completing the previous four lessons? Prepare a 100–250-word report explaining why each of these top ten items have been placed on your list. Save your answer as **Activity 4-1**.

SCANS **ACTIVITY 4-2**

As you conclude your studies of HTML think about the top three weaknesses that you see in HTML. What are the top three things you would change about HTML? What are the weaknesses or things that you feel can be improved? Explain thoroughly in a 100–250-word report how you would like to see HTML become better, easier to use, and more helpful to you as a Web site developer. Save your answer as **Activity 4-2**.

SUMMARY *Project*

Professional Web designers often need to understand and utilize the flexibility of HTML frames to give Web sites the desired appearance. For example, some commercial Web sites are designed with top, bottom, or right-hand navigation bars rather than the left-hand oriented navigation bar presented in this lesson. Using what you learned about frames and frame sets, reorganize the Web site shown in Figure 4-10 so that it illustrates the use of right-hand navigation. Also change the structure of the Web site frames so that the navigation bar spans the full height of the browser window, and the title bar does not span the full width. Your reorganized Web page should look something like Figure 4-14.

FIGURE 4-14
A sample Web site with right-hand navigation

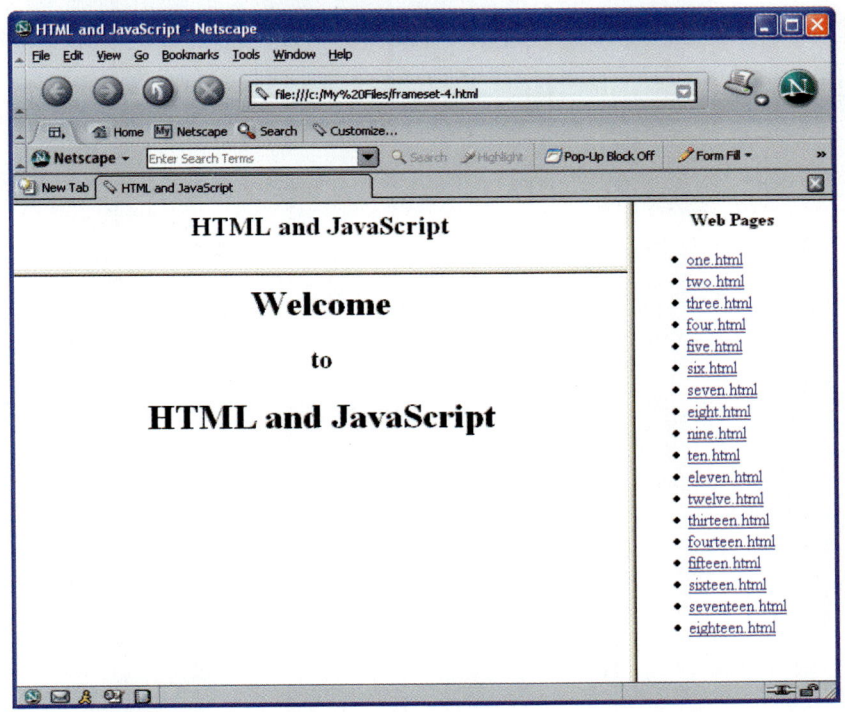

Project Requirements

- You may use the **title.html**, **welcome.html** and **navbar.html** files you created in this lesson to provide the content for your new frame set.

- The upper (title) frame should be about 60 pixels high, and the right (navigation) frame should be about 180 pixels wide.

- Each frame should be separated by a frame border that is <u>not</u> resizable.

- You may want to use concepts from previous lessons (such as fonts and images) to improve the appearance of your title page and welcome page.

UNIT REVIEW

HTML Basics

HTML TAG AND ATTRIBUTE SUMMARY

TAGS OR ATTRIBUTES	RESULT	LESSON
<A> </A>	Creates an anchor tag that is used to create hyperlinks	2
<B> </B>	Bolds text	3
<BODY> </BODY>	Marks text to appear in the body section of the Web browser	1
 	Creates a line or single-spaced break between text	2
<CENTER> </CENTER>	Centers text or graphics on a Web page	1
<EM> </EM>	Emphasizes or bolds text	3
<FONT> </FONT>	Changes the size, font face, and color of Web page text	3
<FORM> </FORM>	Inserts a form set into a Web page	3
<FRAME> </FRAME>	Defines frames within a frame set on a Web page	4
<FRAMESET> </FRAMESET>	Marks the beginning and the end of a frame set	4
<H1> </H1>	Marks text to appear in the largest heading font size	1
<H2> </H2>	Marks text to appear in the second largest heading font size	1
<H3> </H3>	Marks text to appear in the third largest heading font size	1
<H4> </H4>	Marks text to appear in the third smallest heading font size	1
<H5> </H5>	Marks text to appear in the second smallest heading font size	1
<H6> </H6>	Marks text to appear in the smallest heading font size	1
<HR>	Creates a horizontal line between sections of a Web page	2
<HTML> </HTML>	Indicates the beginning and end of a Web page	1
<I> </I>	Italicizes text	3
<IMG>	Displays an image in a Web page	3
<INPUT> </INPUT>	Defines an input control for a form. For example, radio button, check box, text field, etc.	3
<MARQUEE> </MARQUEE>	Creates a scrolling stock market-like ticker	2
<OL> <LI> <LI> </OL>	Marks text for ordered or numbered (1, 2, 3) lists	1
<OPTION SELECTED>	Allows Web developers to define which of a list of options should be selected by default.	3
<OPTION>	Defines an option in a selection list	3

TAGS OR ATTRIBUTES	RESULT	LESSON
<P> </P>	Creates a paragraph or double-spaced break between text	1
<SELECT> </SELECT>	Defines a list of selection options in a form	3
<STRONG> </STRONG>	Emphasizes or bolds text	3
<TABLE> </TABLE>	Used to define tables and table cells in a Web page	3
<TITLE> </TITLE>	Marks text to appear in the title bar of the Web browser	1
<TR> </TR>	Defines a row in a table	3
<UL> <LI> <LI> </UL>	Marks text for unordered or bulleted (•) lists	1
ALIGN=	Aligns text and graphics to the left, right, and center of a Web page	3
BACKGROUND=	Inputs a graphic as a background for a Web page	3
BGCOLOR=	Defines the background color of the Web page	2
BORDER=	Creates a border around the cells in a table	3
CELLPADDING=	Determines the width of the lines separating cells in a table	3
COLOR=	Changes the color of Web page text	3
COLS=	Defines the number of columns in a frame set	4
FACE=	Changes the style or face of the font being displayed. For example, Times New Roman, Arial, or Helvetica	3
HEIGHT=	Changes the height of a graphic	3
HREF=	The hypertext reference attribute. Defines the path or location to a Web page, Internet location, or other online resource	2
LINK=	Changes the color of hypertext links	2
NAME=	The hypertext reference attribute that defines a location on a page, or gives each frame a name	2, 4
NORESIZE	Turns off the option for the user to resize frames	4
ROWS=	Defines the number of rows in a frame set	4
SIZE=	Changes the height of horizontal lines or the size of fonts	2, 3
SRC=	Specifies the source of a resource, like an image to insert into a Web page, or to specify the source Web page to be displayed in a frame	3, 4
TARGET=	Points a Web page or graphic to a specific frame in a frame set	4
TEXT=	Changes the color of text on a Web page	2
TYPE=	Defines the type of input used by a form	3
VLINK=	Changes the color of hypertext links that have been visited or selected	2
WIDTH=	Changes the width of horizontal lines, the width of graphics, or the width of table cells	2, 3

Unit Review HTML Basics

REVIEW *Questions*

MATCHING

Match the correct term in the right column to its description in the left column.

___ 1. The specialized Web language used to instruct Web browsers how Web elements should appear.

___ 2. A Java-like scripting language used to create miniapplications and multimedia effects.

___ 3. Usually appear in pairs enclosed in angle brackets.

___ 4. Operating in base-16, this system uses letters as well as numbers to express values.

___ 5. The definition of attribute.

___ 6. A protocol used to transfer data from Web servers to Web browsers.

___ 7. Graphical format that adheres to international standards; compact enough for Internet use.

___ 8. Graphical format created by a company called CompuServe. The format compresses graphics to transfer over low-speed modems.

___ 9. Term used by programmers that describes a structure, keyword, or tag that contains one or more additional instances of the same item.

___ 10. Software program that makes it possible to avoid having to manually enter every single tag.

A. Dreamweaver
B. gif
C. HTML
D. HTTP
E. Hexadecimal
F. Tags
G. Nested
H. Value
I. jpeg
J. JavaScript

WRITTEN QUESTIONS

Compose a brief answer to each of the following questions. Save the answers in a single file named HTML Unit Summary.

1. List and explain the function of six tags that you believe can be found on most Web pages.

2. List and explain the origin of each of the following file formats. In your explanation, indicate which formats are used for Web pages.
   A. .doc
   B. .rtf
   C. .wpd
   D. .txt
   E. .htm
   F. .html

3. Explain at least two ways in which font size can be increased or decreased. In addition, describe at least two other ways that fonts can be changed.

4. Explain how the anchor tag is used and written to create hyperlinks to sites on the Web and to individual Web pages on your personal computer. In your explanation, indicate how graphics can be turned into hyperlinks.

5. Explain how frame sets work and how Web pages can be targeted to appear in different frames.

SCANS CROSS-CURRICULAR *Projects*

In this exercise you will demonstrate a practical use for HTML. You're going to design a frames page that will help you organize excellent sources of information in at least five academic subject areas. The four required areas are Language Arts, Science, Social Studies, and Math. Pick another subject area of your own choosing, such as Foreign Language, Music, Art, Physical Education, or Technology. Use Web search tools such as *www.yahoo.com* or *www.google.com* to find legitimate academic resources in these subject areas. Choose sites that you will want to return to again and again for information.

This will take some careful thinking and planning on your part. Here's the trick—create a left-hand navigation bar that will access these resource pages for each of these subject areas. Invent your own filenames for your frame set and navigation bar pages. The title bar page is optional. Test all of the links to make sure each one works.

Unit Review HTML Basics

LANGUAGE ARTS 1

Find five Web sites related to the study of Language Arts and place them on a target page that will appear in the right frame of your cross-curricular frames page. Name this file **la-1.html** or **la-1.htm**.

SCIENCE 1

Find five Web sites related to the study of Science and place them on a target page that will appear in the right frame of your cross-curricular frames page. Name this file **sci-1.html** or **sci-1.htm**.

SOCIAL STUDIES 1

Find five Web sites related to the study of Social Studies and place them on a target page that will appear in the right frame of your cross-curricular frames page. Name this file **ss-1.html** or **ss-1.htm**.

MATH 1

Find five Web sites related to the study of Math and place them on a target page that will appear in the right frame of your cross-curricular frames page. Name this file **m-1.html** or **m-1.htm**.

YOUR CHOICE OF SUBJECT 1

Find five Web sites related to the study of a subject of your choice and place them on a target page that will appear in the right frame of your cross-curricular frames page. Name this file **mychoice-1.html** or **mychoice-1.htm**.

SCANS REVIEW *Projects*

PROJECT 1-1

You've probably been thinking, I have created dozens of Web pages, but when can I branch out and create a Web site entirely of my own? Well, now is your chance to harness all of your Web design creativity.

Pick an appropriate topic or theme for your Web site. Using all of the skills you learned in this unit, create an awesome Web site. Invent your own HTML filenames.

PROJECT 1-2

By now, you probably think your Web page is the most awesome site on the Web. And it probably is! However, it's time to find out if that's true! Team up in groups of three or four. Share your Web pages from both the Cross-Curricular Projects and Project 1-1 with your teammates. If any team member is having problems making elements of his or her pages work, solve these problems as a group. Give each other suggestions on how pages can be improved.

SIMULATION

JOB 1-1

Imagine you have just become the lead Web page designer and Web development Team Manager responsible for the GreatApplications, Inc. Web site. To sharpen your team's skills in cutting-edge technology, you have decided to create a Web page cataloging sites that will help your team members learn more about HTML, JavaScript, Flash, and other Web page creation tools such as Dreamweaver, FrontPage, or GoLive. Look at pages you worked on in this unit involving cataloging the HTML learning sites. Add these to your new Web site. Then, reference some of the dominant Web site development companies online, including Macromedia, creator of Dreamweaver and Flash; Microsoft, creator of FrontPage; Adobe, creator of GoLive and other online multimedia tools. Use Net search engines such as *www.yahoo.com* or *www.google.com* to find the resources you need. Invent your own filenames.

JOB 1-2

Do you want a career in the high-tech online industry? If you do, you'd first better find out what types of jobs are available and whether they are to your liking.

Go online and visit some of the major career Web sites such as *www.flipdog.com* or *www.monster.com* and search for ten jobs related to Web page development. If you have trouble finding these types of jobs on these sites, try entering **Online Job Search** into your search engine.

Create a short report that lists all ten of the jobs you have found and explains a little bit about the qualifications you would need in order to take these jobs in the high-tech Web design industry. Save your work as **Job 1-2**.

SUMMARY *Project*

This is your opportunity to demonstrate that you have mastered all of the major concepts in this unit. Consider the information in Table U1-1. This table summarizes the various HTML topics that were presented in the first three lessons.

Your job is to organize this information into a Web page that is laid out as shown in Figure U1-1. Frame A will contain a list of hyperlinks that represent the first three lessons in the book. Frame B will contain its own list of hyperlinks that correspond to the topics covered in one of the lessons. Frame B will be updated each time the user clicks a hyperlink in Frame A. Frame C will contain a Web page that illustrates one of the topics listed in Frame B, and the Web page will change when a user clicks a different link in Frame B. Figure U1-2 shows an example of how the completed Web page might look if the user clicks on Lesson 1 in Frame A, and Headings in Frame B.

Unit Review HTML Basics

TABLE U1-1

LESSON NUMBER	TOPICS COVERED
1	Headings
	Ordered Lists
	Unordered Lists
2	Horizontal Lines
	Background Colors
	Hyperlinks
	Text/Hyperlink Colors
3	Fonts
	Images
	Tables
	Input Controls

FIGURE U1-1
A Web page containing three frames

layout

FIGURE U1-2
An example Web page with Lesson 1 and Headings selected

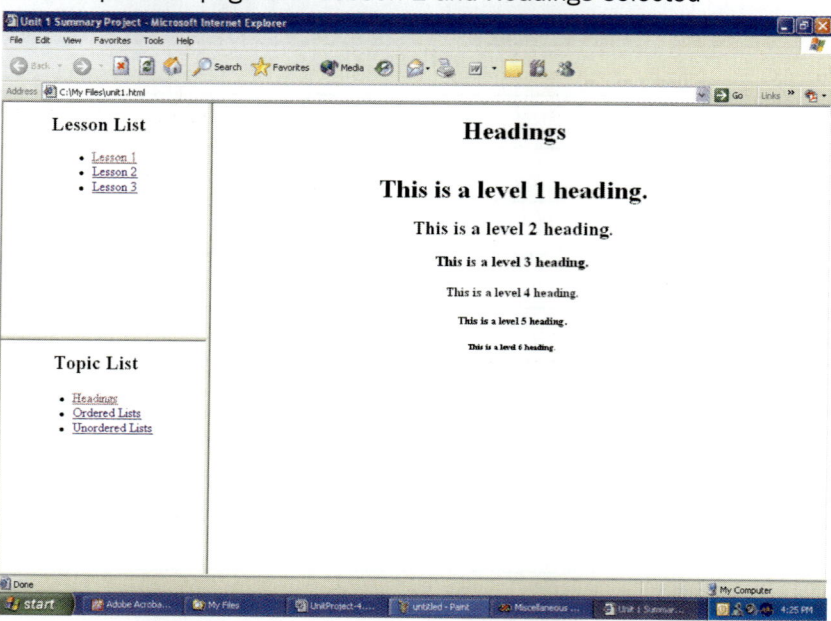

PROJECT REQUIREMENTS

- You must use a nested frame set to create the proper Web page layout.
- Make the two left frames about 25% of the screen width.
- The two frames on the left side should each use about 50% of the screen height.
- Name your main frame set page **unit1.html**.
- You will need to create three Web pages for your topic lists. Name your three files **topics1.html**, **topics2.html** and **topics3.html**.
- You will need to create eleven Web pages for your example pages. Name your files **example1.html**, **example2.html**, **example3.html**, etc.

Unit Review HTML Basics

PORTFOLIO *Checklist*

Include the following files from this unit in your student portfolio:

___ HTML Unit Summary Questions

___ Language Arts 1

___ Science 1

___ Social Studies 1

___ Math 1

___ Your Choice of Subject 1

___ Project 1-1

___ Project 1-2

___ Job 1-1

___ Job 1-2

GLOSSARY

A

Angle brackets HTML tags appear in pairs and are enclosed in angle brackets. The brackets can be found on the comma (,) and period (.) keys on the keyboard.

Attribute Attribute tags are used to enhance an HTML tag. The <BODY> tag is considered an attribute tag because many different types of values are used to change the appearance of the Web page's body or background.

B

Buttons Input controls that are defined with the TYPE attribute instead of the INPUT tag.

C

Check boxes An input control that allows the user to select any or all of the listed options from a set of options.

F

Flash A high impact multimedia creation tool for the creation of Web page content.

Fonts Also known as the style of letters, fonts determine the appearance of text in Web documents. Fonts have three attributes that can be changed—size, style, and color of text.

Frame A rectangular area, a subset of a browser's screen, capable of displaying a Web page that is separate from other frames on the screen.

Frame set tag Allows the definition of a set of rectangular areas on a Web page called frames. Each frame is capable of displaying a different Web page.

G

.gif An acronym for Graphics Interchange Format. GIF files are compact in size and are one of two popular graphic formats used in Web documents. The extension, .gif, alerts the Web browser that these files are pictures, not Web documents.

Graphics Pictures that can be placed in Web documents.

Graphics Interchange Format Compact graphics, also called .gifs, that are small enough to use in Web documents.

H

Hexadecimal Hexadecimal digits operate on a base-16 number system rather than the base-10 number system most people use. Hexadecimal numbers use the letters A, B, C, D, E, and F along with the numbers 0 to 9 to create 16 different digits.

Home page The main Web page for a corporation, individual or organization. A home page is often the first page you see when you start your Web browser.

HTML An acronym for the words *Hypertext Markup Language*.

HTML page An HTML page, or HTML document, is any document created in HTML that can be displayed on the World Wide Web.

HTTP An acronym that stands for *Hypertext Transfer Protocol*. On the location line in your Web browser, this is often seen in the following format: *http://www.course.com*.

Hyperlinks Allow users to click on specific spots in Web documents to link to another page they've created, to another Web page on the World Wide Web, or to another spot within the current document.

Hypertext links Links that transport Web visitors to selected information. Links can be made to information within a document, in another document on the same computer, or to a document residing on any Web server on the Internet. Often used to make Web pages more interesting and easier to navigate.

Hypertext Markup Language Tags created within a Web document that give instructions to a Web browser. These instructions determine the look and feel of a Web document on the Internet.

Hypertext Transfer Protocol The type of digital language that Web servers use to communicate with Web browsers. A protocol is a communications system that is used to transfer data over networks.

I

Internet Explorer One of two major Web browsers used to view information on the World Wide Web. Microsoft Corporation created Internet Explorer.

J

Java A programming language that creates programs called applets. Applets can be added to Web documents using tags similar to HTML text.

JavaScript More powerful than HTML, JavaScript allows Web page developers to add programming features to a Web document without having to know a programming language.

Joint Photographic Experts Group Compact graphics called JPEGs that are small enough in size to use in Web documents.

.jpg or .jpeg An acronym for Joint Photographic Experts Group, .jpg or .jpeg files are compact in size and are one of two popular graphic formats used in Web documents. The extensions, .jpg and .jpeg, tell the Web browser that these files are pictures.

L

Left-hand navigation A narrow left-hand frame that contains hyperlinks that can be used to navigate a Web site.

M

Mosaic The first Web browser that allowed pictures and sound to accompany text on a Web page. Mosaic was created in 1992 at the University of Illinois.

N

Navigation bar A series of hypertext links, usually organized horizontally or vertically on a Web page or in a frame. Used to navigate a Web site.

Nested frame set A term programmers use to describe a structure, keyword, or tag that contains one or more additional instances of the same item.

Netscape Navigator One of two major Web browsers used on the Internet today. Navigator, created in 1994, added to the powerful features of Mosaic, allowing additional features like animated graphics into a Web document.

P

Pixel An individual tiny dot of light inside a computer monitor.

T

Table cell Box in which you can place things to keep your Web document organized. Each table box, or cell, can have different attributes applied to text, can have a different background color, or can contain a different graphic.

Title bar The topmost bar in an open window, or a frame used at the top of the Web page.

U

Uniform Resource Locator Abbreviated as URL, the Internet addressing scheme that defines the route, or path, to a file or program. The URL is used as the initial access to an online resource.

URL Uniform Resource Locator, the Internet addressing scheme that defines the route, or path, to a file or program. The URL is used as the initial access to an online resource.

V

Value Used to define attributes. Values are used in conjunction with attributes. For example, in the tag <BODY BGCOLOR = RED> red is a value used to define the background color attribute in a body tag. The value can be changed to a hexadecimal number such as #0000ff, or words such as BLUE.

W

Web browser Often referred to as a Web client. Allows users to interface with different operating systems and view information on the World Wide Web. It allows Web page developers to have JavaScript compiled and interpreted "on-the-fly."

Web page Any page created in HTML that can be placed on the World Wide Web.

Web site Includes a series of Web pages that can be linked to other Web sites on the Internet. Web sites are stored on Web servers.

Welcome page An introduction page when you visit a Web site. A welcome page often includes the Web page owner's e-mail address and name.

INDEX

A

Adobe, 9, 10, 104
Amazon.com, 82
America Online, 82
Anchor tags, 43
Angle brackets (< >), 4, 56
Artists, Web, 73
Asterisk (*), 93
Attributes, 38, 64–67, 73, 78, 92, 94

B

Background colors, 38–41
Barnes & Noble, 82
Basic tags, 11
.biz sites, 46
Body text (<BODY> tag), 38, 64
Border attribute, 78
Brackets, angle (< >), 4, 56
Break tag (<BR>), 36
Browsers, Web, 3, 6, 16
Bulleted lists, 19–25
Business on Web, 8, 82

C

Careers, Web-related, 73
Case sensitivity, 11
Cellpadding attribute, 78
Cells, table, 78
Cellular telephones, 4
<CENTER> tag, 4
Check boxes, 83–85
Color blindness, 41
Colors
    background, 38–41
    of fonts, 64
    hexadecimal, 42
    text, 54–56
Cols attribute, 92
Communication, 1–8
.com sites, 46
Copyright protection, 76
Corel WordPerfect, 9
Creating Web pages, 33–38
Cyberbusiness, 82

D

Digital images, 73
Document hyperlinks, 42–45

Double spacing, 34–38
Downloading graphics, 67–72
Dreamweaver software, 9, 10, 104
Drive space, network server, 86
Drop-down lists, 83–86

E

E-business, 8, 82
.edu sites, 46
Egghead.com, 82
Electronic tables, 78–82
E-mail, 73
Embedded lists, 25
Ethics, Internet, 44, 76
Extensions, file, 11

F

File extensions, 11
Filenames, 11
Files, text, 11
<FONT COLOR> tag, 64

125

<FONT FACE> tag, 64
Fonts, 34, 64–67
<FONT SIZE> tag, 64
<FONT> tag, 59, 64–67
Frames, 91–93
   advanced options in, 101–104
   nested, 98–102
<FRAMESET> tag, 91–93, 98–99
<FRAME> tag, 91–93
Freeware, 16
FrontPage software, 9, 10, 104

G

.gif files, 63, 67
GoLive software, 9, 10
.gov sites, 46
Graphics, 63–77
   downloading and inserting, 67–72
   font attributes and, 64–67
   sizing, 73–77
Graphics Interchange Format (.gif), 63, 67
Gutenberg, Johannes, 89

H

Headings (<H> tags), 16–19
Height attribute, 73
Hexadecimal colors, 42
Home pages, 9
Horizontal rules (<HR> tag), 38
.htm extension, 12, 93
HTML creation tools, 104
.html extension, 12, 93
HTML Source option, 10
HTML standards, 56
Hyperlinks in documents, 42–45
Hypertext, 34, 46–50
Hypertext Markup Language (HTML), 1–30
   headings in, 16–19
   introduction to, 1–8
   lists in, 19–25
   tags in, 9–11
   viewing pages in, 9, 11–15
Hyptertext Transfer Protocol (HTTP), 46

I

<IMG SRC> tag, 73
Indented lists, 25
Indexes, 34
Inserting graphics, 67–72
Internet ethics, 44, 76
Internet Explorer, 3, 14, 16
Internet Milestones
   e-business, 8, 82
   hexadecimal colors, 42
   HTML creation tools, 104
   HTML standards, 56

J

Java, 3, 9
JavaScript, 3
Joint Photographic Experts Group (.jpg, jpeg), 63, 67
.jpeg files, 63, 67
.jpg files, 63, 67

L

Left-hand navigation, 94
Lines, 38–41
Links, hypertext, 34, 46–50
Link tags, 43
Linux computers, 4
Lists, 19–25

M

MacIntosh computers, 4
Macromedia, 9, 10, 104
Main headings, 16

Index

<MARQUEE> tag, 56
Microsoft, 104
Microsoft Word, 9
Mosaic browser, 8, 16
Mouse cursor, 101
Movable type, 89

N

Name attribute, 92, 94
National Supercomputing Center, 16
Navigation bar, 94–95
Nested frame set, 97–98
Net ethics, 44, 76
Netiquette, 41
Netscape Communications Corp., 8
Netscape Navigator, 3, 8, 14, 16
Net Tip
  case sensitivity, 11
  downloading graphics, 68
  e-mail, 73
  <IMG SRC> tag, 73
  network server drive space, 86
  reload and refresh buttons, 50
  tables, 101
  target attribute, 95
  text attributes, 67
  Web page software, 10

Network server drive space, 86
Notepad, 10
Numbered lists, 19–25

O

Opera browser, 16
Option buttons, 83–85
Options, advanced, 101–104
Ordered lists (<OL> tags), 19–25
Orderly tables, 78–82

P

Pages. *See* Hypertext Markup Language; Web pages
Page source, 6
Palm-sized devices, 4
Paragraph tag (<P>), 36
PDAs, 4
Percentage values, 93
Piracy on Internet, 76
Pixel values, 93
Proofreading, 56

R

Radio buttons, 83–85
Readability, 34

Refresh buttons, 50
Reload buttons, 50
Rows attribute, 92
Rules, horizontal (<HR> tag), 38

S

Saving HTML pages, 11–15
Scanners, 73
Shift key, 56
Shockwave, 9
SimpleText, 10
Single spacing, 34–38
Sizing graphics, 73–77
Slash mark, 56
Software, Web creation, 9
Source attribute, 92
Source code, 6, 10
Spacing, line, 34–38
Standards, HTML, 56
Subdirectories, 47
Subheadings, 16

T

Table cells, 78
Tables, 78–82, 101
Tags, HTML, 4, 9–11. *See also specific tag types*

Target attribute, 94, 95
Text
   attributes for, 67, 73
   coloring, 54–56
   files of, 11
   fonts for, 34
Text boxes, 83–86
Title bar, 99–101
Tools, HTML creation, 104
Type, movable, 89

U

Uniform Resource Locator (URL), 43, 46
UNIX computers, 4
Unordered lists (<UL> tags), 19–25

V

Values, 38, 42, 64–67, 93
Viewing HTML pages, 11–15
Visually impaired persons, 41

W

Web browsers, 3, 6, 16
Web pages, 9, 33–62. *See also* Graphics
   artists and, 73
   creating, 33–38
   document hyperlinks and, 42–45
   examples of, 51–54
   "extras" for, 83–86
   hyperlinks in, 42–45
   hypertext links to, 46–50
   lines and background colors in, 38–41
   proofreading, 56
   tables on, 78–82
   text colors in, 54–56
   welcome, 9, 47, 96–97
Web sites, 9
Welcome pages, 9, 47, 96–97
Width attribute, 73
Windows computers, 4
Word processors, 9

Y

Yahoo!, 82